To Daddy

Woofy woof

Benji

xxx
x.x
x

THE DACHSHUND

Susan M. Ewing

The Dachshund

An Interpet Book

First Published in United Kingdom 2008 by
Interpet Publishing
Vincent Lane
Dorking
Surrey
RH4 3YX

ISBN   978 1 84286 178 3

United Kingdom Editorial Team
Hannah Turner
Nicola Parker

This book has been published with the intent to provide accurate and authoritative information in regard to the subject matter within. While every reasonable precaution has been taken in preparation of this book, the author and publisher expressly disclaim responsibility for any errors, omissions, or adverse effects arising from the use or application of the information contained herein. The techniques and suggestions are used at the reader's discretion and are not to be considered a substitute for veterinary care. If you suspect a medical problem consult your veterinarian.

www.interpet.co.uk

TABLE OF CONTENTS

1

HISTORY

of the Dachshund

The Dachshund is a popular pet in both Great Britain and the United States, and with his two versatile sizes (standard and miniature) and three coat types (Smooth, Longhaired, and Wirehaired), that's no surprise. Add his happy attitude and determination and you've also got a versatile dog for showing, performance events, and hunting. How did we get this wonderful breed?

For those willing to go way back, evidence suggests that dogs began their association with man between 10,000 and 14,000 years ago. Dog historians seem to agree that *Canis lupus*, the wolf, in one form or another, is the ancestor of all the breeds of *Canis familiaris*, the dog, in all the many forms that it takes today. This is pretty amazing when you consider the Kennel Club recognises over 200 breeds and varieties in seven Groups— Gundog, Hound, Terrier, Utility, Toy, Working, and Pastoral—with dogs ranging in size from Chihuahuas to Irish Wolfhounds. There are many more unrecognised breeds around the world.

EARLY DACHSHUNDS

For decades, the Germans bred Dachshunds in three sizes: Teckel, Miniature Teckel, and Rabbit Teckel, rather than just the two sizes—standard and miniature—found in Great Britain and the United States.

The first organised dog show in England was held in 1859, but only Pointers and Setters were entered. By 1870, participants in showing felt that a controlling body was necessary to set basic rules regarding dog shows. In April of 1873, 12 men met in London and founded the Kennel Club.

Although the Kennel Club marks its beginning in 1873, registration records only go back as far as 1908, at which time hundreds of Dachshunds were registered, so there's no way to know the name of the first registered Dachshund. The Dachshund Club was founded in 1881, so the dogs obviously were very popular before the Kennel Club accepted them. In 1927, the Wirehaired Dachshund Club was formed, and in 1929, the

Longhaired Dachshund Club was formed.

World Wars I and II saw a huge decline in both the popularity and population of Dachshunds in both the United States and Great Britain because of the breed's association with Germany. With the perseverance of dedicated breeders on both sides of the Atlantic, as well as the winning qualities of the dogs themselves, the Dachshund's numbers rebounded quickly, perpetuating the breed.

ST. HUBERT'S LEGACY

It is widely accepted that the Dachshund descends from the St. Hubert Hound, a breed that was developed in Ardennes, Belguim by the St. Hubert monks for hunting. St. Hubert (656 to 727 AD), was considered fairly outrageous in his day, rejecting worship on holy days in favour of hunting with his hounds.

One Good Friday, instead of attending church, he set off for a nearby forest. As he was about to shoot a magnificent white stag with his bow and arrow, a cross appeared between the animal's antlers. Hubert immediately repented, and attended church straight away. He confessed his sins, and thereafter led an exemplary life, devoting himself to the church. The monastery, founded in his name, continued to keep and breed hunting hounds long after St. Hubert died.

Tragically, the St. Hubert Hound is now extinct, but there is considerable documentation about the breed. The dog was low to the ground, long bodied and had an excellent scenting ability. Many hounds are believed to have descended from the St. Hubert Hound, including the Beagle, the Basset Hound and the Dachshund.

DACHSHUNDS IN THE UK

England established a Dachshund speciality club even before one existed in Germany. Despite the problems created by World War I, England claimed six noted Dachshund breeders who adhered to a strict breeding code throughout the war. Although these breeders were often referred to as 'pro-German' or 'German sympathisers', they held firm to the integrity of the Dachshund in order to preserve its genetic foundation. Thankfully, their efforts to protect the early gene pool succeeded.

Two of the earliest English Dachshunds to leave an indelible

Dash, the First Dachshund

Dachshunds were originally from Germany and it was Prince Albert who imported Dachshunds into Great Britain. They became very popular during the nineteenth century until the onset of World War I, when it lost its popularity due to its origins.

mark on the breed in the 1890s were Jackdaw, owned by Harry Jones of Ipswich, and Pterodactyl, owned by Sidney Woodiwiss. Those early ancestors still influenced the breed today.

Australia, Denmark, Holland and India are also countries where Dachshunds are popular. In the UK, the Miniature Long-haired Dachshund is the favourite hound, even outnumbering such British hounds as the Basset, the Beagle and the Whippet, the latter being the second-most popular.

THE KENNEL CLUB

Begun in 1873 in Queen Victoria's London a few years after the death of Charles Dickens, the Kennel Club is the main registry for the United Kingdom. The Kennel Club classifies the Dachshund in the Hound Group, for dog breeds originally developed for use in hunting either by sight or scent.

THE AMERICAN KENNEL CLUB

Established in 1884, the American Kennel Club (AKC) also classifies the Dachshund in the Hound Group. The Dachshund Club of America, a member club of the AKC, was founded in 1895. All national breed clubs write the breed's official standard.

FEDERATION CYNOLOGIQUE INTERNATIONALE (FCI)

While many people have only heard of the Kennel Club, American Kennel Club, and perhaps some other national kennel clubs, an international organisation actually exists. The Federation Cynologique Internationale is the World Canine Organisation, which includes 80 members and contract partners (one member per country), each of which issues its own pedigrees and trains its own judges. The founding nations were Germany, Austria, Belgium, France and the Netherlands. It was first formed in 1911 but disappeared during World War I. The organisation was

Hound History

The Dachshund, or Teckel, as he is called in Germany, has been known since the Middle Ages and is thought to have evolved from dwarf mutations of taller hunting hounds, possibly the Schweisshund or the Bibarhund, with possible crosses with terriers and/or spaniels to obtain the wire and long coats.

The Ever-Popular Dachshund

The Dachshund has been among the top ten most popular dogs based on registration with the American Kennel Club for decades. In the United Kingdom, the Kennel Club breaks down Dachshund registrations by both size and coat type. In 2006, the miniature Longhaired Dachshund was 41st in popularity; the Smooth-coated mini was 31st; and the Wirehaired mini was 56th. The Wirehaired standard held 82nd place; the Longhaired standard came in 98th; and the Smooth-coated standard Dachshund was in 99th place.

Today's Dachshund breeders understand the importance of breed type and temperament, just as early devotees of the Dachshund did.

reconstituted in 1921. Currently, neither the United States or Canada is a member.

The FCI ensures that its pedigrees and judges are recognised by all FCI members. Every member country holds international shows as well as working trials; results are sent to the FCI office , where they are input into computers. When a dog has earned a certain number of awards he can receive the title of International Beauty or Working Champion. These titles are confirmed by the FCI. The FCI recognises 331 breeds, and each of them is the "property" of a specific country, ideally the one in which the breed developed. Each breed's owner country writes its breed standard, in cooperation with the Standards and Scientific Commissions of the FCI; the translation and updating are carried out by the FCI. In addition, via national canine organisations and the FCI, every breeder can ask for international protection for his or her kennel name.

HOW REGISTRIES SUPPORT BREEDERS

Both the Kennel Club and the American Kennel Club support purebred dogs by serving as registries for dogs and setting rules and regulations for competitive events, which in turn serve as showcases for each particular breed, as is evidenced by this quote from the Kennel Club: "The basis of breed shows is the judging of dogs against the 'Breed Standard', which is the prescribed blueprint of the particular breed of dog. For all licensed breed shows, the Kennel Club Breed Standards must be used for the judging of dogs. The Kennel Club owns the Breed Standards, and all changes are subject to approval by the Kennel Club General Committee. New Breed Standards, for newly recognised breeds, are drawn up once the breed has become sufficiently established within the UK. Careful research is conducted into the historical

National breed clubs encourage proper breeding through guidelines and special programs for their members. This helps Dachshund breeders—and owners—understand and value the Dachshund.

Fanciers participate in dog shows around the country and around the world that are sanctioned by organisations like the American Kennel Club in the US or the Kennel Club in the UK.

The American Kennel Club

The American Kennel Club (AKC), founded in 1884, is the most influential dog club in the United States. The AKC is a "club of clubs", meaning that its members are other kennel clubs, not individual people. The AKC registers purebred dogs, supervises dog shows, and is concerned with all dog-related matters, including public education and legislation. It collects and publishes the official standards for all of its recognised breeds. Their website offers many informative pages relating to breed standards.

background, health, and temperament of any new breed before Kennel Club recognition is granted."

The AKC mission statement says that the American Kennel Club will "maintain a registry for purebred dogs and preserve its integrity, sanction dog events that promote interest in, and sustain the process of, breeding for type and function of purebred dogs. Take whatever actions necessary to protect and assure the continuation of the sport of purebred dogs.

The Dachshund Club

The Dachshund Club was founded on 17th January 1881, making it the oldest breed club for Dachshunds in the world, and one of the first clubs for any breed. The original British breed standard was drawn up, based on the German standard. This was revised jointly with the Northern Dachshund Association in 1907. Originally only catering for Smooths, the only variety known in Britain at the time, the other five recognised British varieties were taken under the Club's wing as they came into the country.

The first Championship show was held in 1946, in fact two were held that year. It was not until 1989 that CCs for all six varieties were allocated to the Club, a situation that remains today, making the Dachshund Club the only breed club to run an individual show with CCs available for all six varieties.

The Club was instrumental in setting up Dachshund Rescue with the Long Haired Club in 1972.

The Dachshund Club Handbook is eagerly awaited and held in the highest regard world wide. Published every three years the complete volume dates back to 1946. The Club also distributes a newsletter annually, and holds the copyright to 'Sayers Standard of Points' considered the definintive extended breed standard.

The Dachshund Club was one of the first breed clubs to introduce judges training in 1968 with the judging trials, now developed into a formal Dachshund Breed Judge Assessment Scheme.

The Dachshund Club has a Code of Ethics, which it expects all members to follow:

- To discourage indiscriminate breeding, bearing in mind always the welfare of the bitch as a primary consideration and the long-term welfare of any puppies that are bred.

- To ensure that puppies sold knowingly to any dealer or pet shop do not breed from any Dachshund that has, or may carry, any serious hereditary faults. In particular, not to allow any dog to be used at stud if he has, or could carry, any serious hereditary faults and to be very selective of the bitches on which he is used.

- To enjoy and applaud other people's success, be welcoming to newcomers and ensure as best as possible that dogs behave quietly on the bench.

- That, as a judge, to act with courtesy and integrity to all exhibitors, will judge according to the standard of points and to consider as part of any decision the temperament and physical condition of the dogs judged.

C h a p t e r

2

CHARACTERISTICS

of the Dachshund

There's no mistaking the Dachshund. Both standard and miniature Dachshunds and all three coat varieties are judged by the same "standard," which includes references to the three coat types. No matter what size or variety, this long-in-body and short-of-leg dog is a bold, confident, intelligent, and alert companion. The Dachshund was bred for hunting, flushing out game, and if necessary, following his quarry into a den or burrow. He has a good nose and a loud bark, making him ideal for trailing and for letting the hunter know just where he is.

HOW A STANDARD DEFINES A BREED

A standard is a written description of a purebred dog. It's like a blueprint for breeders, telling them what "perfection" is in any given breed. No dog is perfect, of course, but all responsible breeders do so with an eye to the standard of perfection, trying to make each generation of dog better than the one before.

The Kennel Club approves the standard of each breed it registers. If you read the standard of a purebred dog, you will have a good idea of what the dog should be like, even if you've never met that particular breed. The standard will describe the build of the dog, starting with the head. Should the dog's ears stand straight up, or hang down? How long or short is the nose? Is there a preferred shape of eye? You'll find the answers in the standard, which can be found on the Kennel Club website, www.the-kennel-club.org.uk

THE STANDARD AS A BLUEPRINT FOR THE BREED

The standard will tell you what the correct proportions of a specific dog should be. Corgis and Dachshunds, for example, are longer than they are tall, while Pugs should be more square-shaped. Many standards will make reference to the purpose for which a dog was bred. If you want a dog to pull a sled for miles at a time, you want a dog with strength and a good coat. Although Dachshunds have strength, a smooth coat would not survive in the frozen north, and those short legs wouldn't cover much ground.

The Dachshund was developed as a hunting dog, and the standard reflects that. There

The Dachshund Standard

If you're reading this book to see if a Dachshund is right for you, read the entire standard on the Kennel Club website, www.the-kennel-club.org.uk. If you've already chosen your Dachshund, read the standard anyway and see how close your dog comes to the ideal. Remember, though, that no dog is perfect, and if you're not planning to breed or show your dog, a fault doesn't matter if it doesn't threaten the dog's health. So what if your pet is a little long in the leg or has a less-than-perfect tail? Enjoy his wonderful personality, and be thankful every day that you have a Dachshund.

is an emphasis on a strong jaw with full dentition. The chest must allow enough room for the lungs to retain oxygen when the dog is working underground. No matter what his coat type, a Dachshund should still have the instinct to hunt, as well as the nose and voice that goes with that instinct. A Dachshund is built to go into burrows. Those short, strong legs help to push the dog into the tunnel, and the keel-like breastbone also helps as he goes after his prey.

A standard also will describe the temperament of the breed, and this is perhaps the most important information of all. Dachshunds may be small, but they were bred to hunt badgers, which means they are not timid. They will stand up for themselves, even if that means not backing down from a larger dog. They can be

Dachshunds come in two sizes (standard and miniature) and three varieties (Smooth, Longhaired, and Wirehaired). This photo shows a Smooth with a Longhaired Dachshund.

fearless and may try to be a bit bossy. Says the AKC standard, the Dachshund is "clever, lively, and courageous to the point of rashness, persevering in above and below ground work."

The Dachshund was developed as a hunting dog, and his entire structure supports that purpose, from his strong jaws to his short legs.

Making Changes to the Standard

The system varies from the United Kingdom to the United States. In the UK, the Kennel Club owns the Breed Standards and all changes are subject to approval by the Kennel Club General Committee. Breed Standards for newly recognised breeds are drawn up once the breed has become sufficiently established. The background of the breed, as well as health and temperament, is researched before Kennel Club recognition is granted.

The Dachshund Club of America is in the process of considering changes to the AKC breed standard regarding piebalds and double dapples. A revision is not something that is easy to do. A committee generally works on whatever revision may be suggested, and then the revised standard is voted on by the club membership. Rules vary within each club, but frequently, standard revisions need to be approved by two-thirds of the membership.

Did You Know?

The Dachshund can have three different types of coat, smooth-haired, long-haired or wire-haired.

15

THE DACHSHUND'S PHYSICAL FEATURES

Everyone knows the basic "long and low" shape of the Dachshund, but there's more to the Dachshund than that. Let's start at the tip of the nose, which should be black. Then, let's travel back over the tight lips, where there is no drooling with a Dachshund. Those lips cover a strong jaw, with equally strong teeth. Remember, the Dachshund is a hunting dog who needs to be able to deal with whatever prey he is after. Those teeth meet in a scissors bite, and anything other than a scissors bite is a fault. The muzzle is slightly arched, and there's very little stop between the muzzle and the skull.

Next come the eyes, dark rimmed and almond-shaped. The eyes are very dark and should have an "energetic, pleasant expression." The Dachshund's ears are set near the top of his head and are medium length and rounded. When the dog is animated, the forward edge of the ear just touches the cheeks so that the ears frame the face.

Now, follow the slightly arched neck down to the Dachshund's shoulders. The long Dachshund back runs in a straight line from the withers, and the abdomen is slightly drawn up. The Dachshund may be short, but he's not droopy. His skin is loose to prevent tearing as he tunnels into a burrow.

The Dachshund's ribs are well sprung and oval-shaped, allowing plenty of room for the heart and lungs, and the breastbone is prominent in front. Long, broad shoulder blades, an upper leg at a right angle to the shoulder blades, and short forelegs, all covered

A Dachshund has a black nose, tight lips that cover a strong jaw, a slight stop between the muzzle and skull, and dark-rimmed, almond-shaped eyes.

with strong muscle, make him an ideal digging machine. The joints between the forearms and the feet are closer together than the shoulder joints, so the front does not appear absolutely straight. The paws are full, tight, and compact, with well-arched toes and tough, thick pads. They may be equally inclined slightly outward. Front dewclaws (the fifth toe above the heel) are usually removed.

The Dachshund may be short, but he's not droopy: the standard calls for a long back, a slightly drawn-up abdomen, and well-muscled hindquarters.

The Dachshund's hindquarters are also strong and well muscled. All the joints form a series of right angles, and from the rear, the thighs look strong and powerful. When viewed from behind, the back legs are upright and parallel. The hind paws are a bit smaller than the front paws, again with arched toes and tough pads. The hind foot points straight ahead. Rear dewclaws should be removed.

The tail is a continuation of the spine and should have no kinks, twists, or curves. Long ago, hunters used that long, strong tail as a handle, a way to grab onto and haul the Dachshund out of a burrow or den.

The Dachshund in Motion

When talking about movement in Dachshunds, it's a good idea to remember that they were bred as hunting dogs. Movement should be smooth and the forelegs should reach well forward, without much lift, in unison with the driving action of the hind legs. There's no wasted energy in this kind of movement, and dogs who are out in the field trailing game need to conserve energy. The legs do not move in exact parallel planes but incline slightly inward to compensate for shortness of leg and width of chest.

Hind legs drive on a line with the forelegs, with hocks straight. If the dog is moving correctly, the rear pads should be clearly exposed during rear extension. Feet must not swing out, cross over, or interfere with each other. Short, choppy movement or a rolling or high-stepping gait are both faults. The working Dachshund needed agility, freedom of movement, and endurance to do his job, and breeders still strive for those ideals today.

Colours

When it comes to colour, Dachshunds have quite a variety. Many Dachshunds are red, ranging from a light red, which may appear reddish blond, to a rich, deep shade of red similar to that of an Irish Setter, with or without a shading of interspersed dark hairs. Cream is also an accepted colour, though rarely seen. A small amount of white on the chest is acceptable but not desirable.

Two-coloured Dachshunds include black, chocolate, wild boar, gray (blue), and fawn (Isabella), each with tan markings over the

Red, black, and tan are common Dachshund colours.

Dachshunds also come in piebald and dapple colour patterns.

eyes, on the sides of the jaw and underlip, on the inner edge of the ear, front, breast, inside and behind the front legs, on the paws and around the anus, and from there to about one-third to one-half the length of the tail on the underside. Wild boar is a combination of light and dark hairs that gives the dog a salt-and-pepper appearance. Again, there may be a small amount of white on the chest.

There are also dappled Dachshunds. The "single" dapple pattern has lighter-coloured areas contrasting with a darker base colour. Both colours should be equal in area. A larger patch of white on the chest of a dapple is allowed. A "double" dapple is one in which varying amounts of white colouring occur over the body in addition to the dapple pattern.

Piebald (patches of black and white or other colours) is not a recognised colour pattern in the Dachshund standard. The piebald gene is recessive and doubles the white gene, which can result in eye and ear problems. If this is the colour you want or already have, ask the breeder about any health issues that exist or may come up. Double dapple also can result in serious health issues such as small eyes, no eyes, or hearing issues.

Brindle is a pattern (as opposed to a colour) present in some

Dachshunds in which black or dark stripes occur over the entire body, although in some specimens the pattern may be visible only in the tan points.

Coat Types

Now let's look at the three coat types. A Smooth Dachshund has a smooth, close coat, which shouldn't be very thick, although long bristles may show up on the dog's underside. However, this is not a fault. The tail should be covered with hair, but it shouldn't have any hint of fringe.

In Wirehaired Dachshunds, with the exception of the jaw, eyebrows, and ears, the whole body is covered with a uniformly thick, rough, hard outercoat and a finer, somewhat softer, shorter undercoat distributed between the coarser hairs. The absence of an undercoat is a fault. Wirehaired Dachshunds also have a beard and eyebrows. On the ears, the hair is shorter than on the body and is almost smooth. There should be no soft outercoat anywhere on a Wirehaired Dachshund, and no long, curly, or wavy hair. The tail should have lots of hair and should gradually taper to a point. The most common colours in a Wirehair are wild boar, black and tan, and shades of red, but all colours are allowed.

If you have a Longhaired Dachshund, you have a dog with

The Longhaired Dachshund has sleek, longer hair; the Smooth has a short, close coat; and the Wire has a thick, rough outercoat and finer undercoat as well as a defined beard and eyebrows.

Learn as much as you can about all aspects of the Dachshund before deciding if it's really the breed for you.

a sleek coat of longer hair. Longer, slightly wavy hair is usually found under the neck, on the chest, on the ears, behind the legs, and on the underside of the body. The hair is longest at the tail. Too profuse a coat, equally long hair over the whole body, a curly coat, or a pronounced parting on the back are considered faults.

ARE YOU READY FOR A DACHSHUND?

Take the time to find out all you can about Dachshunds before you make a commitment that could last 14 to 16 years or more. Talk to breeders and owners. Ask a veterinarian questions. If possible, go to a dog show, watch Dachshunds in the ring, and talk to handlers. Try to do all of this before you actually get a Dachshund puppy.

Presumably, if you're at the stage where a puppy is crawling into your lap, you've done some homework and are seriously looking for an addition to your family. If you aren't already looking, take a minute to think about what having a puppy means. Do all the members of the family want a dog? If there are children, their vote is probably yes. They may even say they will take care of the dog. They may even mean it, but depending on their age, they may not be able to do everything for the dog. They might eventually ignore the unpleasant aspects of dog care or lose interest after the novelty has worn off. It's up to the adults in a family to

The Dachshund's Temperament

Although there are slight differences in temperament among the varieties, and even from dog to dog, generally speaking the Dachshund is a lively dog who is "courageous to the point of rashness." This can get him in trouble, as he will not hesitate to confront dogs much larger than he is, but it also makes him a wonderful watchdog.

Who wouldn't find these puppies irresistible? Their charm doesn't make them the right breed for everyone, however.

commit to the care of the dog for his lifetime. If the person who will be the primary caregiver doesn't really want a dog, then a dog is not a good idea. If the adults in the family want a dog and are willing to take care of that dog's needs, from food and water to housetraining to necessary visits to the veterinarian, not to mention playtime and exercise, then it's time to choose the right Dachshund for your family.

Grooming Requirements

For starters, there's the question of coat. If you get a Dachshund, you will be getting hair in varying degrees. Even the Smooth Dachshunds shed. The hairs are short and work their way into carpets and upholstery. Longhaired Dachshunds will require more grooming to keep mats from forming, and the Wirehaired variety also will require grooming to keep them looking neat and tidy. Think about how much time you want to spend grooming, or if you want to consider regular trips to your local groomer.

Temperament

The Dachshund is often described as being corageous and lively, often rash. This is why a fenced garden is so important. If a Dachshund picks up the scent of a rabbit or squirrel, he's going to follow that scent, and he's not going to be paying attention to oncoming traffic if that trail should happen to cross a road.

Dachshunds aren't usually afraid of bigger dogs, either, even when they should be. It's fine for your Dachshund to play with other dogs, but make the introductions gradually, and be sure everyone wants to play and is friendly. If the dog is much bigger than your Dachshund, be cautious. A large dog can easily harm a smaller one, even by accident.

Like all dogs, Dachshunds know how to get what they want, and they're so cute that it's hard not to give in. But don't let that cute little puppy sleep at the foot of the bed or curl up on the couch next to you if you won't want the adult doing the same thing. If you intend to let your adult sleep with you, fine, but if not, don't allow your dog to develop the habit as a puppy.

While Dachshunds are hunting dogs and happy to follow a trail, they are also very much "people" dogs. They need to be a part of the family, not shut away in their crates or left out in the garden.

Low, but All Go

Dachshunds are short, but they have a bold nature, and they won't hesitate to launch themselves from your bed or the couch or even a grooming table. If, for whatever reason, they are up on a relatively high surface, help them to the ground. Constantly jumping down from high places can lead to back and shoulder injuries. If you enjoy having your Dachshund with you on a high bed or couch, consider building or buying a doggy ramp.

Physically, Dachshunds are short and don't weigh much. This means that you can pick them up if you have to, which can be an advantage when your dog is sick and can't jump into the car on his own for that trip to the veterinarian's office. They are sturdy enough, though, to play with children and not get injured if the play should get a little rough, although children should be taught to always be gentle with the dog.

Your Dachshund and Training

The character of the Dachshund has been described as intelligent, happy, self willed, and affectionate. The intelligent, and self-willed parts of your Dachshund mean you should definitely consider some obedience training, even informally, or your Dachshund soon will be trying to run the household. You may never want to compete in formal obedience trials, but it's always a good idea to teach your Dachshund some basic commands. While you can learn how to do this in Chapter 6 of this book, a good class also will help you to socialise your Dachshund, getting him used to other people and dogs.

Their small size makes it convenient to pick Dachshunds up and carry them. Help them up and down from high places so they don't injure their backs.

Exercise Requirements

Your Dachshund will need some daily exercise, of course, but definitely not as much as a larger dog. Indoor games can give your Dachshund some exercise, and a brisk walk down the road a couple of times a day should do just fine. If jogging is your favourite activity, though, you should know that Dachshunds are not built for long runs. While they certainly can (and do) cover ground when hunting, running is not their best trait.

Dachshunds need daily exercise; in a fenced garden or enclosed area, a run off-lead is a joy for your dog.

If you have a Smooth coat, consider a doggy sweater in the winter months when your Dachshund is outdoors exercising. If you have a fenced garden, never leave your Dachshund unattended for long. In the summer months, make sure there's shade and plenty of water available. If you don't have a fenced garden, keep your Dachshund on a lead; a loose Dachshund is a lost Dachshund.

Dachshunds are more than willing to cuddle on the couch, but they're even more willing to be active. Some Dachshunds will retrieve toys for as long as you'll throw them. Some will entertain themselves in the garden chasing squirrels, and some want a nice, brisk walk to check out all the sights and sounds of the neighbourhood. Whatever they do, Dachshunds like to do it with their people!

Eating Requirements

Dachshunds are chowhounds. They love to eat and can look quite pathetic when you're having a snack and they're not. The amount of food a Dachshund will need will depend on how active he is, so you may need to do a bit of adjusting before you discover the right amount of food. A miniature may only need half a cup a day, while a standard may need a cup. (More on feeding in Chapter 4.)

Once you determine the right amount for your dog, try to stick with that amount. Overweight animals can suffer poor health, just like overweight humans. They can develop joint problems,

A Dachshund's needs and personal characteristics will determine his suitability to your lifestyle.

heart disease, and diabetes. The occasional bit of cheese or leftover scrambled egg won't kill your Dachshund, but don't overdo it, and unless you want to turn your lovable Dachshund into an annoying pest, don't ever feed him from the table.

Watchdog

If you're looking for a watchdog, the Dachshund may be the perfect choice. A Dachshund will definitely let you know if someone knocks on your door, and he'll keep letting you know until you do something about it.

An instant way to frighten off an intruder or alert you to the arrival of the postman!

Sociability

With Pets

If you have other pets, make introductions gradually and your new dog will fit right in. Dachshunds and cats *can* be friends, especially if introductions are made when your Dachshund is a pup. If your Dachshund is an adult and you're bringing home a kitten, control all meetings between the dog and cat, and make the introductions gradual. You might want to start with the cat in a room with a closed door and let the animals sniff each other through the crack. With the first face-to-face meeting, keep the dog on a lead and always make sure that the cat has an escape route or a high shelf for safety.

If you already have a dog, be cautious when introducing your new Dachshund. Choose a neutral place for the first meeting. Keep both dogs on lead, but try to keep the leads loose. A tight lead can tell the dog there is something to fear and can lead to aggression. Think about the temperament of the current dog. Talk to the breeder or others who may have a Dachshund in a multi-dog household. Generally, if the other dog is friendly, the Dachshund will be just fine.

Although two males may not get along, your Dachshund should be able to live with other pets in the household. Whether it's another Dachshund or some other breed, if the dogs are introduced properly, you shouldn't have a problem. While an individual Dachshund may get along with individual guinea pigs, birds, hamsters, or even mice, remember that all of these animals would ordinarily be prey for the dog predator in the wild. This is why it's important never to leave any dog alone with any small pet without supervision.

Dog toys appeal to dogs because the toys make a high-pitched squeaky sound. Small, furry animals make a very similar sound. Keep those other pets safe, even if your Dachshund seems inclined to be friendly. Remember that your Dachshund was bred to be a hunter.

With Children

Most children will ask for a dog at some point, and most parents, if it's possible, will want to get their child a dog. Getting a family dog can be a wonderful experience, but remember, even if the child says the dog is hers, and even if you agree that the dog "belongs" to the child, in reality, you are responsible for the care and welfare of the dog. Children will promise anything to get a dog. They'll promise to feed him and brush him and walk him, and they may mean it. In the beginning, they may even do it, but sooner or later, something will come up, and they won't have time or they'll forget. It's up to you to make sure the dog gets his walk or his dinner, no matter where your child is.

A dog is a living entity, not a way to teach your child responsibility. So give your child some responsibility in caring for the dog, but remember that she is not necessarily going to be able to meet all the dog's needs. Trips to the veterinarian is one area beyond the ability of your child. Housetraining may be another area.

A child in school is not going to be able to successfully housetrain a puppy. Housetraining takes patience, persistence, and a parent. Realise that however much the child wants him to be "her" dog, he is also "your" dog. If you are not prepared for that responsibility, you should wait a bit before you add a dog to your home.

Just as some breeders will not sell to anyone with an unfenced garden or a pool, some will not sell to families with small children. Dachshunds can be wonderful with children, but sometimes very small children have a hard time distinguishing between a live puppy and a stuffed toy, and many Dachshunds will take exception to rough play.

Any Dachshund can be a wonderful dog for a child, but no matter what variety you select there are things to think about:

Did You Know?

"Spurlaut" is the German word for the high, shrill, distinctive, piercing, and insistent bark of a Dachshund when he spies prey (or something he thinks is prey).

Living Little

The Dachshund makes an ideal dog for a flat because of his small size and low exercise requirement.

Is your child old enough and mature enough to understand that the puppy you've brought home is a living creature who can be frightened and hurt? Has your child shown that she can be gentle and careful with a puppy? Will there be an adult to supervise interaction between child and dog? Dachshunds are small and can be loving and playful with children, but the general rule is to never, ever leave a baby and a dog alone. Babies make sudden movements and high-pitched noises, just like prey. Dogs were and still can be predators, especially dogs bred to hunt. Don't *ever* leave a baby and a dog together unattended.

Children have seemingly endless amounts of energy. Puppies may seem very energetic, but they also need their rest. Make sure that your child understands that there is playtime and then there needs to be rest time. Enforce this. Having a crate can make this much simpler. It's easier to pop a tired

A Dachshund can be an exceptional companion for a child, but remember, responsibility for the dog's daily needs will probably fall to the parents.

While they will love playing together, puppies—like children—need time to rest.

puppy into a crate and shut the door, letting the child know it's nap time, than to try to convince the child to stop playing with the puppy and let him sleep.

How Do Dachshunds Get Along With Children?

Generally speaking, Longhaired Dachshunds are very good with children, Wirehairs are good, and Smooths are fairly good. This is obviously a generalisation, but Longhaired Dachshunds tend to be a bit more laid back; the Wires are more playful and ready to go; and the Smooths are a bit more aloof.

Chapter

3

PREPARING

for Your Dachshund

There is no single hard and fast rule for choosing the Dachshund puppy who will be right for you and your family. My best advice is to listen to the breeder or person from whom you are getting your puppy. That person should want the best possible match between a puppy and his new owner. Just as not every breed is right for every person, not every Dachshund is right for every person. Be honest with your source so that everyone is happy.

WHERE TO FIND YOUR DACHSHUND

Breeders

Because your Dachshund will be a member of your family for 14 to 16 years, take the time to make the right match. Start with finding a breeder you can work with. The Kennel Club can supply you with details of a reputable breeder in your area, who is a memeber of their Accredited Breeder Scheme. Talk to several breeders. A person may be a wonderful breeder, but if you're not comfortable talking with her, find someone else. You want to be able to contact this breeder when you have questions about your Dachshund. The most valuable thing a breeder can give you, besides the puppy, is her phone number—and her time.

Another place to find a breeder is at a dog show. All exhibitors are listed in the back of the catalogue, and the list includes their addresses. Talk to the Dachshund people at a show and ask questions about temperament, grooming, and exercise. Watch the Dachshunds in the ring. If one catches your eye, maybe you can get a related puppy. Just remember, at a dog show, while you may be able to exchange a word or two ringside before the dog is shown, save the long conversations for after the handler and dog have been in the ring. Before judging, handlers are concentrating on their dog, and may be abrupt if you start asking questions. Talk to them after they've shown and the odds are good they'll be more than happy to help.

Those breeders who breed champions like this dog can tell buyers all about their puppy's ancestry so they know what to expect physically and temperamentally.

Breed Rescue

Rescue organisations are another source to explore. Just because a dog is in rescue doesn't mean there is anything wrong with him. It may be that someone hasn't done the homework necessary for selecting a particular breed of dog. They may have gotten a Dachshund puppy and found he needed more attention than they could give, or the dog needed more exercise than they expected. A divorce may mean the family dog is surrendered to rescue, or someone in the family may be allergic to dogs.

As cute as puppies are, there can be advantages to getting an adult, and this is when a rescued dog is especially appropriate. For one thing, an adult will probably—although not always—be

Health Tests for Dachshunds

Hip dysplasia can occur in any breed, and while people tend to think of it as more of a problem in large breeds, it can occur in small breeds as well. The Kennel Club and the British Veterinary Association (BVA) run a scheme together, the aim of which is to find the presence of any signs of hip dysplasia. If this is a concern of yours, choose your puppy from stock that has had its hips tested. Many breeders do thyroid checks on their breeding stock as well. Ask if your puppy's parents have been tested. Did the breeder check the adult Dachshunds' eyes before breeding? With miniature Longhairs, especially, progressive retinal atrophy (PRA) can be a problem. Many breeders of standard Dachshunds will also test for PRA. Some breeders also test for von Willebrands disease, a bleeding disorder.

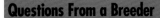

Questions From a Breeder

Responsible breeders of any breed will ask many questions of prospective buyers, either on the phone, in person, or in writing. Be prepared to honestly answer questions like these:

1. How did you hear about us?

2. How did you become interested in Dachshunds? Do you know someone who owns one?

3. If you own or have owned a Dachshund in the past, please let us know from whom you obtained your dog. If it was some time ago that you had the dog, when was it?

4. Have you read any books about the breed? If so, which ones?

5. What are your expectations for your dog? Pet, show, companion…what words would you use to describe what you would like in a dog?

6. Do you have a preference for a male or a female puppy? Would you take a puppy of the opposite sex should your first choice not be available? If not, what creates the preference?

7. Would you be interested in an older puppy or an adult?

8 Tell us a bit about your household. Do you have a spouse, partner, or roommates? How many children and what are their ages?

9. Do any family members suffer from allergies?

10. Who will be responsible for the care and training of your pet?

11. Would you call your family more the "outdoors-type" or "homebodies"?

12. In what family activities would you include your dog?

13. Have you ever had a dog before? Do you have any pets at this time (other dogs, cats, birds, fish, etc.)? Please tell us a little bit about your previous pet-owning experiences.

14. Do you have a veterinarian your family uses or has used in the past? If yes, please provide the name, address, and telephone number.

15. Do you live in a house, townhouse, flat or apartment? If so, how large is your garden and what type of fencing do you have?

16. If you rent, are you allowed to have a dog? Please provide the landlord's contact information.

17. Have you thought about how you will handle your dog's exercise needs? Please describe.

18. In what rooms inside your home will your dog be permitted? Do you have any ideas about how you will keep your dog out of certain parts of your home, if necessary?

19. Have you thought about housetraining a puppy and handling an adult dog? Where will your dog go to relieve himself? How will you clean up?

20. How many hours each day will your dog be left alone while you're at work? Do you have a secure place to leave your pet while you are away from home? Where will your pet sleep at night?

21. If travel plans took you away from home, what arrangements would you make for your dog? Boarding kennel? Pet sitter? Neighbours or relatives? Take your dog with you?

22. Training and proper socialisation are important to a puppy's development into a secure and happy adult companion. Can you devote the time needed during the critical first few months to teach manners and expose your puppy to many new experiences? Do you have any ideas about where you would go for obedience training or socialisation?

It's a long list, but you can see that responsible breeders want the best for their puppies, and they want to make sure that you understand exactly what is involved in owning a Dachshund. Answering these questions and reviewing the considerations presented in Chapter 2 will help you to think about your puppy's needs and just how you will meet them. With luck, the puppy you choose will be a loving companion for many years.

housetrained. As adults, they also can wait longer before having to go out. This means you can skip the housetraining stage and may not have to worry as much about accidents in the house. Another advantage to an adult is that he will probably already know some basic commands. He will have outgrown the puppy urge to chew everything in sight. The dog also will be spayed or neutered, as it is very rare for a rescue organisation to let any dog go to a new home without this being done.

Conversely, an adult may come with habits or problems that you will have to learn about and deal with. It could be something minor, like having to teach the dog he is no longer allowed on a couch, or it could be something more serious, like a dog who is food aggressive, or is afraid of children. While most rescue organisations have the dogs in foster care to determine just what, if any, problems there might be, animals shelters usually don't have the staff or the time to be able to assess the potential problems. You may trade housetraining time for retraining time.

A rescue organisation will ask as many questions as a breeder. They want to find a permanent home for their charges. Don't take offence at these questions. They want the best match possible between dog and family, and they want the placement to last. A rescue dog may already have been in two or three homes, so the rescuers will be determined to find him a permanent home.

WAITING FOR THE RIGHT DOG

No matter what source you try, don't expect to get a dog immediately. If you're trying to get a puppy from a breeder, understand that responsible breeders are probably not going to have more than a couple of litters a year. When you call, they may not be planning to have any puppies for six months or more. Also, breeders frequently have waiting lists for their puppies. Even being on a list doesn't guarantee you a puppy. If there are five people waiting and there are only two puppies, three families are going to be disappointed.

Don't be too firm about what you want, either. Don't demand a black female or nothing at all. What if all the girls in the litter are red? What if there are no girls?

There's not much difference between male and female Dachshunds. A male will housetrain as easily as a female but may lift his leg against furniture as a way to mark his territory, especially if exposed to intact females. Neutering at an early age usually (but not always) prevents this. If the dog is a show prospect, you may not neuter while showing, and this means you will have to be ready to deal with this behaviour if it starts. With females, unless spayed, you must deal with twice-yearly heat cycles. If you are not planning to show, both sexes should be neutered. This will not affect their personalities and will make

A Dachshund rescue organisation may be able to pair you with an older dog who will be just right for you and your family.

them much easier to live with as pets.

Listen to your source and be flexible. I guarantee that a dog is going to worm his way into your heart just as quickly whether male or female. Having said that, don't let yourself be talked into a puppy you just don't want. No matter what the outcome of the temperament test or the breeder's assessment of which puppy would be best for your household, if you know you never will be able to deal calmly with a leg-lifting male, hold out for a female. It may mean a longer wait or going to another breeder, but when you choose a puppy, it should be for life.

Pet or Show Quality?

Do you want a pet-quality or a show-quality puppy? These two terms likely will be in the contract you and the breeder sign. Neither term should have anything to do with health or temperament. Your puppy should be in good health and have the proper Dachshund temperament whether you want a pet or whether you want to show your dog. Calling a dog "show-quality"

You should receive the puppy's Kennel Club Registration Certificate from the breeder.

If you're patient and do your homework, when you finally get your Dachshund you'll know you were meant for each other.

is not a guarantee that the dog will ever become a champion. "Show-quality" means that the dog meets the standard and has no serious faults that would hinder him from winning. A show-quality Dachshund will have a proper bite, will not be any colour that's not allowed, and will otherwise conform to the standard.

A pet-quality Dachshund may have a tail that is set too high. The ears may be set too low or too high. His feet may stick out too far. These things would make it hard, if not impossible, to win in the conformation ring, but none of these would stop the dog from being a loving family companion, or from being able to compete in many of the performance events. A breeder also may call a puppy "pet-quality" even if he meets the standard physically if he doesn't have the personality for the conformation ring.

The price for a pet-quality puppy is usually less than the price for a show-quality puppy. Also, the contract will call for the pet puppy to be spayed or neutered, which helps ensure that a buyer will not breed what a breeder considers a pet quality dog.

No matter what kind of registration the breeder offers, those registration papers should be given to you when you get your puppy. If you're in the UK, the Kennel Club will be the registry. In the United States, the dog will most likely be registered with the AKC, but it might be registered with the United Kennel Club. If your puppy is from Canada, the papers should be from the

Finding the Perfect Match

A responsible seller is going to try to make the best match between you and the puppy. It may be that for your lifestyle, the red male is a better match than the black female. A trainer I know once spoke of a particular dog, saying, "Would he be my choice for a family that had never had a dog before? No. Would he be my choice for obedience competition? Absolutely."

Bonding With Your Dachshund

Many people think that if they don't get their puppy as young as possible that the dog won't bond with them. This is not true. Older puppies are very adaptable and will quickly adopt and love new humans as quickly as the new humans adopt and love them! Most adult dogs will transfer their love and loyalty to their new family as well, so if you're considering an older rescue dog, don't hesitate because you're afraid you won't bond.

Canadian Kennel Club. Contact information for these and other registries can be found in the Resources section.

How Old Before He Can Come Home?

The age at which a puppy should go to a new home is a frequently debated question. Many breeders refuse to let a puppy go before eight weeks, and many prefer to keep their puppies until they are twelve weeks old, starting the crate training and housetraining and making sure that the puppies have all the necessary vaccinations before they go to their new homes.

READYING YOUR HOME FOR THE NEW ARRIVAL

No matter where you get your Dachshund, make sure you're ready for him before you get him, especially if you're bringing home a puppy. Check electrical cables and tape them down or tuck them safely away from an inquisitive puppy. Decide what rooms will be off limits. If those rooms don't have doors that you want shut, invest in baby gates for doorways. An adult dog may come with a bed or a crate, but if you're getting a puppy, get a crate before he arrives. Crates are a wonderful way to keep your puppy safe, make housetraining easier, and give your puppy his own little den.

Beds

There are so many wonderful types of dog beds on the market that you'll be tempted to buy several. Until your Dachshund is an adult, however, you might want to stick with old towels or flannel sheets. These can make a perfectly wonderful, cosy, warm bed. They are also inexpensive, so if your Dachshund decides to chew them, you won't be out a lot of money—and you won't be angry at your puppy; after all, he's just being a dog. Towels and flannel sheets are easy to wash, and puppies are likely to have accidents. Many beds are washable, but drying a foam bed can take hours. Even with a dryer, many won't dry completely and need to be air-dried for two or three days. Crates can make great beds that double as a den, too. They'll be discussed in greater detail later in the chapter.

Regardless of the type of bed you choose for your Dachshund, it's a good idea to put the bed in a place where it'll be convenient

and practical for your friend to use it. That means putting beds in places you frequent with your family—the kitchen, the den, and of course, your bedroom. Unless you are vehemently opposed to your Dachshund sleeping in the same room with you, you all will be happier with him there. With his own comfy spot, he won't be tempted to join you in your bed.

Collars and Leads

These are absolute necessities, and before you buy something purely because it looks nice, remember that these items must be functional as well as attractive. Collars that are too heavy or bulky may even harm your puppy or dog. Leads that slip out of your hand, or are too thin, too thick, or too fancy will soon have you frustrated when you need to simply control your dog on a walk.

Remember, too, that your puppy will grow. You may want to outfit him in a cheaper nylon collar until he's reached his adult size and you can invest in a leather collar that may last the rest of his life. Many puppy collars today are made so that the buckle tongue can be pushed through the fabric at any point, making it easy to expand the collar as the puppy grows.

Measure your puppy's neck before you buy a collar, or better yet, bring him along to the pet shop so you can select one that meets all your criteria right away. The same goes for a lead.

In It To Win It

Successful show dogs need to look alert and lively in the ring. A dog who hates to show, who lags at the end of the lead, is not going to win, no matter how gorgeous he is physically.

39

Make your dog's sleeping areas practical and comfortable so you don't risk something fancy getting soiled or chewed.

Look at the different sizes and styles and "test drive" the ones you like. A basic 6-foot lead made of cotton, nylon, or leather is a safe selection.

Identification Tags

The Control of Dogs Order 1992 stipulates that all dogs that are in a public place must wear a collar with the name and address (including the postcode) of the owner engraved or written on it, or on a tag. It is optional, but advisable, to include your telephone number. You can be fined up to £5,000 if your dog does not wear an identification tag.

As important as a clear ID tag is, any tag could come off or be removed from a dog's collar. A permanent way to identify your dog is by having him tattooed and/or microchipped. Dogs can be tattooed with a special number that's put on the inside of their thigh or ear. They also can get a microchip implanted in the muscle between their shoulder blades. The microchip is about the size of a grain of rice and contains a special number that belongs to your dog. A special scanner can read the number and then a veterinarian or shelter worker can check with the microchip registry and locate you. No matter what you choose, be sure to use some form of identification. If your Dachshund should get lost, proper identification may mean the difference between that

loss being permanent or getting your dog back.

Food and Water Bowls

Invest in a good set of dishes—ones that are easy to clean, won't slip when you put them on the floor, and aren't made of potentially harmful materials. Stainless steel is relatively inexpensive and can be thoroughly cleaned. The stainless steel food and water bowls are typically lined with rubber on the bottom to prevent skidding. There are lots of adorable ceramic bowls out there, too, but be sure that the paint or glaze is not lead based. Hard plastic is not a great choice because it may be chewed on and possibly swallowed. In addition to being destroyed, it also may harbour germs, and the material itself can become toxic over time.

Your dog will need one bowl for food and a separate bowl for water. The bowls should be cleaned before and after use, just as yours are. Cool, clean water should be offered at all times, and the water should be changed several times a day.

Toys and Chews

Because puppies love to play and chew, you should get toys that are appropriate for the size of your puppy. A toy that's too small can get stuck in a dog's throat. A toy that's too big may not be easily enjoyed. My dogs have always loved stuffed toys with squeakers, but they also love ripping the toy open to get at the squeaker. I have to supervise play so that when the toy is torn open, I'm there to remove all the stuffing. I don't want the dogs swallowing mouthfuls of that synthetic fibre. I pull it all out and the dogs get the "shell" of the toy, the outer fabric cover. Some dogs never destroy a stuffed toy and will carry it around for years. Just keep an eye on your dog until you know which kind he is.

Dachshunds are notorious chewers, and their desire to chew needs to be satisfied. If you don't choose something appropriate, your dog will choose something inappropriate. Hard nylon and rubber chews often can keep a Dachshund occupied for hours at a time. There are even toys you can stuff with goodies that make them even more appealing. Rotate your Dachshund's toys and chews, too, so he doesn't get bored.

Just remember to supervise play and make sure toys don't have any sharp parts. If it's a stuffed toy, check any added parts, like floppy ears or bows. Keep playtime safe and happy.

Bedding Care

Keep your dog's bedding clean. Wash it separately as often as you wash your own linens to keep them clean. Your dog may not care, but you'll notice a difference.

Puppies enjoy chewing on rope toys and other appropriate chews.

REGISTERING YOUR DOG

The registration process with the Kennel Club is similar to that of the AKC. If a breeder has a litter to register, he contacts the Kennel Club or downloads the necessary form from the Kennel Club website. After completing the form and sending it with the proper fee to the Kennel Club, the breeder will receive a litter registration certificate and one registration certificate for each puppy in the litter. When the breeder sells a puppy, she signs and dates the Breeder Registration Certificate and gives it to the new owner with other documentation. The breeder should encourage the new owner to complete the Change of Ownership and return it to the Kennel Club. After the new owner has sent in the paperwork, The Kennel Club sends back a registration certificate and a booklet, *Giving Dogs a Good Home*, which provides general information on the Kennel Club and the world of dogs.

Registering With the American Kennel Club

A purebred dog is eligible for American Kennel Club registration if his litter has been registered. When you purchase a dog said to be AKC-registrable, you should get an individual registration application from the seller. Once the application has been completed, you should submit it to the AKC with the proper fee. You will receive your dog's AKC registration certificate in about one week. This must be filled out jointly by the litter owner and the new owner of the dog. The application is colour-coded for the convenience of both parties. The litter owner must fill out most of the application, including the sex of the dog; colour and markings; type of registration (either full or limited); date of transfer; the name and address of the new owner or owners and any co-owners; and the litter owner or owners must sign the form.

As the new owner of the dog, you must supply the name of the dog, sign the form, note method of payment, and check any options you may want, such as your dog's official AKC pedigree or any videos. When the application has been received and processed by the AKC, the registration certificate will be posted to you. Examine it carefully and report any errors to the AKC.

Each person or firm who owns, breeds, or sells dogs who are AKC-registrable must keep accurate, up-to-date records of all transactions involving the dogs. There must be no doubt as to the identity of any individual dog or as to the parentage of a particular dog or litter.

Dogs from other countries may be registered with the AKC, provided the dog is registered with another recognised kennel club. For instance, a Canadian dog must have an unrestricted registration with the Canadian Kennel Club. A transfer of ownership on the AKC's records only will be affected after it is documented that the same change has been made by the registry organisation in the owner's country of residence. Application for a foreign-bred dog must be accompanied by an official three-generation pedigree.

The Benefits of Registration

Of course, your Dachshund will still be your loyal pal whether you manage to register him or not, but if you are planning to compete in any Kennel Club conformation shows he'll need to be registered. If he isn't registered and you wish to take other KC events, such as agility or obedience, he'll need to be registered on the Activity Register.

Registering of Imported Dogs

If you want to register a dog that has been imported with the Kennel Club, the dog must already be registered in the country of its origin. Registration is normally only accepted from overseas countries where there is a reciprocal agreement with the overseas Kennel Club or from countries that have full

What is the Activity

Any dog from any background may be registered in the Activity Register. Any dog on this Register may then compete in activities licensed by the Kennel Club, such as Obedience, Flyball, Working Trials, Agility and Heelwork to Music. It will not be able to compete in Field Trials or Gundog Working Tests.

When driving with your Dachshund in the car, make sure he is secure at all times.

membership, associate membership or contract partnership of the FCI (Federation Cynologique Internationale). Further information can be found on the Kennel Club Website www.the-kennel-club.org.uk.

TRAVELLING WITH YOUR DACHSHUND

Whether it's a trip to the shops or a trip across the country, travelling with your Dachshund should be enjoyable for everyone. Most enjoy a ride in the car, although some may get a bit carsick as puppies. Carry a roll of paper towels with you and you can easily clean up after the little one.

To ensure that your pet always will be a willing traveller, start when he's a puppy to get him used to the car. Take him for short rides that don't always end at the veterinarian's office. How eager would you be to get in the car if you always ended up at the doctor's office? Take the puppy with you when you drop off the kids at school as well. Not only will this be a happy car ride, it's a good way to socialise the puppy at the same time. Any time you can take the dog with you, do it. Reward him with treats when he jumps in the car. Soon you'll have a dog who begs to go with you every time you pick up your car keys.

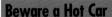

Beware a Hot Car

When the sun is shining, the interior of a closed car can reach dangerously high temperatures very quickly. Never take your dog with you if he's going to have to stay in a closed car for very long. Even in the autumn and spring, when the outdoor temperature may seem pleasant, if the sun is shining, the inside of the car can reach lethal temperatures. Parking in the shade may not help because as the sun moves, your car may no longer be in the shade. Windows can't safely be left open very far if your dog is loose in the car; Dachshunds can get through surprisingly small openings, and they will. Even if your dog is crated, you might not want your windows all the way down. So, think ahead. If there's even a chance that the dog will be left in a hot car, leave him at home.

Putting your Dachshund in a crate for car rides will help keep him safe, but there are other ways to restrain your dog in the car, including special harnesses that attach to the seat belt. What you use is your choice, but use something. Dogs riding loose in the car can distract the driver, and Dachshunds are small enough to get between the driver's feet and the pedals. In an accident, a Dachshund can be seriously injured, and if not injured in the actual crash, he may escape from the car into traffic. Even if there's not an accident, Dachshunds are quick. Open the door for just a minute to run into the shop, and your Dachshund may be right beside you or out in the middle of the road. Restrain your Dachshund for safety.

Holiday Considerations

When holiday time rolls around, it will be time to decide if you want to take your Dachshund along, board him, or use a pet sitter. If you're driving and you want to have your dog with you, plan ahead. Will the dog be allowed at your destination? Will the dog be allowed at any of the places you may be stopping along the way? If there will be overnight stays at hotels, call ahead and make sure your pet will be welcome. Some hotels will charge an extra fee for a pet. The fee may or may not be refundable. Some hotels will agree to a dog if the dog will be crated and if he is never left in the room unattended. Find out what the rules are before you arrive at the hotel. The advent of the Internet has made checking out various hotels much easier, faster, and cheaper.

If you're planning on stopping at attractions during the trip, call ahead to those, too. Otherwise, think about where your dog will be while you're enjoying the water slide. Remember, leaving the dog locked in a hot car is *not* an option. If your entire holiday is going

to be visits to parks and museums, a boarding kennel or pet sitter may be a better idea for your Dachshund.

If your travel plans include camping, make sure your campground accepts dogs. Find out the rules *before* you go.

Packing for Your Dog

If your dog will be travelling with you, you'll need to pack for him as well as for the family. Take a small first-aid kit, as well as some water for your dog. If you'll be on the road longer than a few days, mix local water with your dog's water so he gets used to the change gradually. Carry dog food. Unless you're absolutely sure it is a kind you can get at your destination, make sure you carry enough for the entire trip. Suddenly changing foods on top of the stress of travelling can lead to digestive upsets.

Make sure your dog is wearing his collar and tags. If you're going to be at your destination for a week or more, you might want to have a tag made with the local phone number on it, or the number of someone who will know how to reach you no matter where you are in your travels. If your dog is on any medication at all, take enough to last for the length of the trip. Do you use a monthly flea preventative? Add that to your bag.

I always carry extra towels. Dachshunds love splashing through puddles, and because they're short, this means that their undersides get as dirty as their paws. A few extra towels can protect your car and your clothes. Towels make good beds, too. If you don't want to carry food bowls, a paper plate works just fine and can be thrown away instead of being washed.

Carry cleanup materials with you at all times and *pick up after your dog*. No one, not even another dog lover, wants to step in a mess left by your dog. Pick it up. There are all kinds of products on the market that make this easy. There's even one that fastens

Hotel Etiquette

If you're staying more than a night or two in a hotel, you should consider tipping the housekeeper at the beginning of your stay rather than at the end. This can make whoever cleans your room a bit happier, or at least a bit more willing to vacuum up those Dachshund hairs — and let's face it, there will be Dachshund hairs.

Your Dog's Travel Kit

My dogs' travel bag contains a couple of inexpensive dog bowls, a couple of toys, dog treats, a long lead for exercise if there's a large open space, and two old sheets for covering the beds in hotel rooms. When we're at home, the dogs don't sleep on the beds, but when we travel, they love to jump up and be with us while we're reading or watching television. Rugs can be vacuumed, but bedspreads are not washed after every guest, and dog hairs have a way of working into the threads of a bedspread. Be considerate and spread out a towel or sheet. This also prevents mud and water from being transferred from your Dachshund to the bedspread. If you don't want to carry your own, ask the housekeeping staff for a sheet. They'd rather launder an extra sheet or two than have to deal with a hairy bedspread.

Your dog's crate and collar with identification tags are some of the staples you'll need before setting off on a trip together.

onto your dog's lead. With Dachshunds, a small plastic sandwich bag works just fine. Turn it inside out over your hand, pick up the waste, pull the bag forward over it, twist shut, and deposit in the nearest rubbish bin. There are even some biodegradable bags on the market that may be safely flushed.

I also travel with a lightweight folding crate for each dog. The hard-sided crates stay in the car for travel, and the mesh crates go into the hotel room. They're much lighter and easier to carry, especially if you're on the second floor and there's no lift. A few towels on the floor of the crate make it cosy, and your dog has a safe spot when you're not in the room. Crating your dog in a hotel room is a good way to prevent any damage to the room. A piece of plastic under the crate, or at least under the food and water dishes, will cut down on stains from any accidental spills.

To keep your Dachshund looking and smelling his best during your travels, be sure to pack towels and other clean-up items.

I can't stress enough the need to leave your dog crated in a hotel room, but I also know that on rare occasions, there will be a dog who just can't tolerate a crate. If that's the case, put out the "do not disturb" sign. You don't want someone coming to clean your room and letting your dog escape. You also don't want your dog barking or growling at whoever opens the door.

Flying With Your Dog

You may, of course, be flying to your holiday destination, and that requires different thought. Every airline is different, and the rules change frequently, so check with your specific carrier, so there'll be no surprises. All airlines have limits on when they will fly dogs as cargo and some may have a limit as to how many they will accept on any given flight.

If your dog will be flying as baggage, you will need an airline-approved crate. Plastic may be a better bet than metal because

Making a Home Away From Home

If you must leave the dog in the room alone, turn on a radio or television. This will mask noises that might otherwise cause your dog to bark. No one wants to listen to your dog bark while you're out enjoying yourself. My dogs are very good about being left alone, but I did have one once who was not so good. She frequently barked when left alone. Our solution was to take her with us when we went out to dinner. Of course, if you have a barker and the weather is hot, dinner will have to be at the drive-thru window of a fast food restaurant.

metal tends to absorb more heat. Tape a label on the crate that lists your destination, your name, address and telephone number, as well as your dog's name. You might also want to include your veterinarian's phone number. Make sure there is absorbent bedding in the crate. Shredded paper is a good choice. Freeze water in the water dish so that your dog can either lick the ice, or drink the water as the ice melts. This prevents the water supply from spilling

Make sure to notify your airline beforehand if you will be flying with your dog.

Your dog may look pathetic when you leave him at the kennel, but harden your heart and walk away. The odds are good that he'll quickly adjust, and if the kennel operator offers a dog biscuit or two, your Dachshund will make a new friend in record time.

all at once. You also may want to run a bungee cord over the door to prevent it from opening if the crate is dropped.

Check with airline personnel about how and when your dog will be loaded and where and when you can pick him up when the flight lands. Plan your route carefully. Plane transfers will be harder on your dog, especially if the plane heats up or the crate is left on the blacktop in the sun. There is also more of a chance that he can get lost en route. If you are travelling in very hot weather, the airline may refuse to fly your dog at all. The optimal temperature range, and frequently the range the airlines use, is 45°F to 85°F (7.2°C to 29.4°C) . If it will be colder than 45°F or warmer than 85°F at either the originating airport or your destination, or any place in between that the plane may land, most airlines will refuse to ship your dog.

If you don't actually see your dog being boarded, ask the gate counter agent to call the ramp to make sure your dog is on board. Pick up the dog promptly at your destination. If you don't get your dog in a reasonable amount of time, ask about him. Ask before your plane has taken off again.

Bringing Minis On Board

Most miniature Dachshunds are small enough for soft carriers that will fit under the seat in the cabin. Airlines generally limit the number of live animals they will allow in the passenger section, and they charge for this service, so make your arrangements ahead of time. Don't just arrive at the airport with your dog in his carrier.

If you've decided that you do want to try to take your dog on the plane with you, make sure he's used to the carrier before the trip. Feed him in the carrier and take him on short car rides while he's in it. If he's crate trained, you shouldn't have too much trouble, but the soft dog carriers are smaller than crates, so there will be a bit of

adjustment necessary.

Choosing and Using a Boarding Kennel

I love having my dogs with me, but sometimes I want the freedom to sightsee without having to get back to feed or exercise them. I want to stay up late and not have to get out of bed at 6 a.m. to walk the dogs. That's when I make arrangements for my dogs to stay at a boarding kennel. If you do your homework, you should have no qualms about leaving your dog behind at a kennel. Sure, they'd rather be with you, but they'll be safe and well cared for in a kennel.

This does not mean that you don't still have some work to do before you leave your dog. Visit the kennel ahead of time. Take note of the fencing and the runs. The fencing should be in good repair, with no bent pieces of wire that could injure a Dachshund. The runs should be clean. There may be a doggy odour or the odour of a cleaning product, but it shouldn't smell of urine or

Most kennels allow pairs of dogs to share a run and spend their time together.

If you want to bring bedding to the boarding kennel, choose something durable and easy to clean, like an old bedspread or towels.

faeces. There should be water in the runs. If there are dishes in the runs, what do they look like? Are they clean?

I prefer a kennel where the walls separating the runs are solid on the bottom to prevent contact between the dogs, but I would not reject a kennel where the runs were separated only by chain-link fencing, if everything else met with my approval. Ask about drop-off and pick-up times. For an extra fee, some kennels offer a pickup and delivery service. Do they give baths? Dogs pick up a definite kennel odour with an extended stay at a kennel. I like mine to get a bath and have their nails trimmed before they come home.

Many kennels have an exercise garden where dogs have more

room than in their run. If you have more than one dog, this gives them a chance to play together. Ask about the kennel's policy regarding putting strange dogs together. Many dogs get along quite well, but if you don't want your dog socialising with others, or you know your dog doesn't get along with other dogs, tell the operator. It's always better to supply too much information, rather than too little.

Specific Concerns

Some kennels also will offer extras in the way of individual walks on lead and possibly basic training. If you have a very active Dachshund, a daily walk might be a good idea.

Will the staff give your dog any necessary medications? There may be an extra charge for this. What do they do in an emergency? Most kennels will ask for your veterinarian's name, but in an emergency, they may use one they know or someone closer to the kennel. Tell them your preference. When I board our dogs I always request that any problem be treated aggressively. I would rather pay a veterinary bill for a false alarm than have something serious overlooked.

Once you've chosen a kennel, it might be a good idea to plan a short practice visit for your dog. Board your dog for a couple of nights. This will give your dog a chance to get to know the kennel and the kennel operator, and your dog also will learn that you will return. Also, the younger your dog is, the more easily he will adapt to a kennel. A dog who is 10 or 12 years old the first time he is boarded is not going to adjust as quickly as a young dog.

If you have more than one dog, many kennels will let your dogs share a run, often at a reduced price. If you decide on this option, make sure your dogs will get along together if they are fed in the confined area of a run. Possibly the kennel operator will agree to feeding them separately. Again, find this out ahead of time.

To Bring or Not to Bring

You may want to take your dog's crate to put into the run, especially if the runs do not have a solid barrier between them. That way your dog can have a private space, which may help until he adjusts to the kennel. Many people like to take their dog's bed to a kennel, and it's a nice thought. My recommendation is an old blanket or rug you don't care about, or several old bath towels.

Taking a Toy

While the idea of your dog having his favourite toy with him is a comforting thought, for the most part, dogs in kennels don't play with their toys much. Also, a toy or bone that is fine at home where you are supervising your dog may not be a good idea in a kennel run. Most people who run kennels will remove anything they consider unsafe, but it's your decision. If the toy or bone is questionable, leave it at home.

These items can be easily washed, and if the dog destroys them, it's no great loss. I've seen lovely, expensive wicker baskets, as well as bean bag beds and beds stuffed with foam, be totally destroyed. An anxious dog may be a destructive dog.

The kennel will supply the dishes and water buckets, so leave yours at home. The kennel owner has probably already chosen a dry food that seems to agree with most dogs. If your dog is on a special diet, or you don't want him to change foods while being boarded, most operators will allow you to supply your own food. Do not expect a discount for this. Food is a very minor part of what you're paying for, and as a former kennel owner, I know that it is much easier to feed everyone the same food, rather than fixing several dogs special meals, especially if that special meal includes dry and canned food, supplements, hard boiled eggs, and other items. I was always willing to do whatever the owner wanted to keep the dog happy and healthy, and most kennel operators feel the same, but to suggest they take less money for more work is not appropriate.

Pet Sitters

Another option is to hire a pet sitter. With a pet sitter, your dog remains in your home. He is familiar with the house and

garden, and especially for an older dog, there will be less stress. Pet sitters will come in from two to five times a day for varying lengths of time. They will walk your dog at your request or play with the dog for a few minutes. Pet sitters are more expensive than a boarding kennel, but there is the advantage that someone is in and out of your home, possibly even watering your plants and bringing in your mail. Most importantly, your dog will be in familiar surroundings. If you have an old dog or a dog with any medical problems, using a pet sitter might be a better choice than a boarding kennel.

As with a boarding kennel, if you want to use a pet sitter, make arrangements before you need them. Talk to sitters about the times you would expect them to visit. Find out how they handle emergencies. Are they willing to give medications? What experience have they had, and with what kinds of dogs? Check references. Once you have settled on a sitter, have her visit your home to meet your dog *before* you go away. Two or three meetings are even better. You want both your dog and the sitter to be comfortable with each other.

No matter what option you choose, keep your dog's health and safety in mind when you're planning your holiday.

C h a p t e r

4

FEEDING

Your Dachshund

Food is a very important part of your Dachshund's life, as he'll be sure to let you know! But no dog can choose his own diet, and it's up to you to make sure you feed your Dachshund the very best in nutrition, keeping him healthy and helping him live a longer life.

There was a time when no commercial dog foods were available. Dogs lived on what their people lived on. They ate table scraps and the occasional bone from the butcher. There was no specific balanced diet for dogs. Now, the aisles in the shop are lined with all kinds of dog foods and treats. Our dogs eat balanced meals every day, and the diet is consistent. Interestingly, some people now advocate the earlier type of diet, with daily variety, raw bones, and even more "people" food.

With all the choices today, what is the best food? The supermarket shelves are full of all kinds of dog foods in all different forms. There are big bags of dry food, packets of semi-moist foods, and rows and rows of tinned food. Beyond that, many dog owners prefer cooking for their dogs, and many more have chosen to follow the BARF diet, which stands for Bones And Raw Food, or Biologically Appropriate Raw Food.

Your puppy's breeder probably gave you information about your puppy's diet and, at first, you should follow those guidelines. If your breeder is feeding a premium dry dog food, you should, too. If she prefers tinned, or raw, or home-cooked food, she's probably given you information to help you do the same. As your dog grows, you may find you want to try something else.

Whatever you feed, make sure you understand what your dog needs to stay healthy, and what specific diets require. Also, when changing foods, do it gradually, over a period of about a week, to prevent stomach upsets or diarrhoea. (The exception to this may be if you are switching from commercial to a BARF diet, when a clean break may be preferred.)

Your Dachshund will look forward to his meals, and with the variety of foods available today, it's important that you choose what's best for your dog.

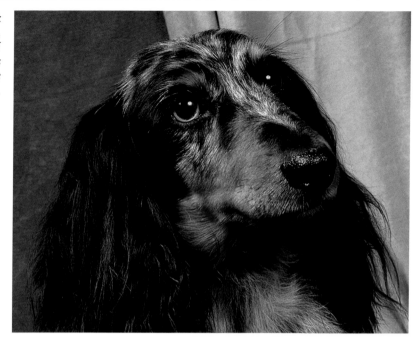

Your Dog's Response to Food

Observe your dog and see how he responds to his food. Does he eat it quickly and seem to enjoy it? Check his stools: are they firm? Is his coat in good condition, or is it dull or brittle? No matter what type of coat your dog has — Long, Smooth, or Wire — your Dachshund's coat should have the lustre of good health.

READY TO GO

About 10 years ago, it was estimated that nearly 95 percent of owners fed their dogs pre-prepared dog food products. While that number may have declined in recent years, due to owners who have started making their dog's food themselves in order to control the quality of ingredients or provide a specific diet, it is still likely that the huge majority of owners feed their dog a food that they have purchased ready made. Read the label and check the list of ingredients. Two of the first five ingredients should be an animal-based protein and, ideally, one of those should be in the first position. Chicken, beef, and lamb are the usual kinds of meat you'll find listed. Next, how much filler is there? Corn is cheap, but many dogs are allergic to corn. One breeder I know stays away from any product with wheat in it, but I look for wheat, rather than corn. Some dogs react negatively to soy. This will be trial and error, but it is something to be alert to.

Another thing to pay attention to when selecting a food is the type of preservative used. Many people look for a food preserved with vitamin E (listed as tocopherol). What you need to remember about "natural" preservatives is that they will not preserve the food as long as some other preservatives, so you will want to buy smaller quantities of the food.

Look to see if the dog food you're choosing contains "meat by-products." This may sound unappealing, but, in fact, may be very good for dogs. Meat by-products are the lungs, liver, kidneys, spleen, heart, intestines, stomach, etc.—the organs that are always the first to be eaten by wild dogs and cats. Chicken by-products also include the head and feet of the bird. Organ meats are extremely high in natural vitamins and minerals. Many people prefer to feed only real meat to their dogs, but by-products don't necessarily indicate poor ingredients.

COMMERCIAL DOG FOOD OPTIONS

Commercial food offers several options to the dog owner. Dry food (kibble) is the most convenient, economical, and sound choice and should be the base of your Dachshund's diet. Dry food gives dogs something hard to chew, which helps keep their teeth clean, though most dogs tend to gulp their food rather than do any sustained chewing. The advantage to dry food is that it will not stick to the teeth as easily as semi-moist or tinned, thus keeping the dog's mouth a bit cleaner.

Semi-moist food is more expensive than dry. It is soft and

Food Allergies and Your Dog

If your dog is scratching, if his skin seems dry and flaky, or if he is chewing at his paws, he may be allergic to something in his food. A trip to the veterinarian will rule out other causes, and if it appears that a food allergy is the problem, your veterinarian will help you determine what the source is.

You may want to try a raw or home-cooked diet for your Dachshund.

Puppies weaned on softened kibble have no problem adjusting to regular kibble, which makes for a nutritionally sound food base.

frequently moulded into shapes designed to please people. Some of it may look like ground meat because of added dyes. Read the label. It may contain more of the things you may want to avoid, like preservatives and sugars and starches, which are added for texture, flavour, and aroma.

Tinned food is the most expensive choice, but it contains more meat, and most dogs find the smell, texture, and taste irresistible. But again, read the label. How much of what is in the tin is just filler? Many owners mix a small amount of tinned food with a base of kibble so their dogs are getting a nutritionally sound meal with the added bonus of tasty tinned food.

Premium dog foods offer a balanced diet for your dog, with necessary vitamins and minerals. If you feed a balanced food, you shouldn't need supplements. Commercially prepared foods are the easiest, cheapest way to feed your Dachshund.

Assessing Brands

There are dozens of brands of dog food on the market, and while many are high quality, not all are right for every dog. Even within a breed, one brand may be too rich for an individual dog, or not be well tolerated by a dog. If you plan to feed a commercial diet, study the labels, ask your breeder, ask friends, and observe your dog. If he is not itching or chewing on himself, if his coat is glossy and healthy-looking, if he is growing well and is not too fat or too thin, and if his stools are small and firm, chances are you're feeding him an appropriate food.

NON-COMMERCIAL DIET OPTIONS

All-natural diets are gaining in popularity, as are home-cooked meals. If you decide to prepare your Dachshund's food yourself, be aware that he still needs a balanced diet. Cooking up some ground meat or chicken and adding some boiled rice may be fine to help correct the occasional upset stomach, but it is not a balanced diet. Bones with the meat attached are not balanced. There is also a concern about bacteria in raw meat and eggs, and about splintering and other effects from bones. Some veterinarians are totally against feeding raw meat because of the health threat of salmonella and *E. coli*; others say that the benefits outweigh the possible danger. People who feed raw claim their dogs have shinier coats, cleaner teeth, and fewer health problems.

Serving Bones to Your Dog

Very few dogs have problems with fresh bones, but some do, and pounding or grinding the bones can help prevent problems.

Cooking for Your Dog

Cooking for your dog and meeting nutritional standards means adding vegetables as well as vitamins and minerals. There are some excellent books on the subject of natural feeding versus commercial foods. If this is what you prefer, research the subject thoroughly. Two books that may help are *Give Your Dog a Bone,* by Dr. Ian Billinghurst, and *Raw Dog Food*, by Carina Beth MacDonald.

Your veterinarian may not approve of a raw diet, but see if he

Consider varying your dog's diet to keep his system used to different ingredients.

Your dog's activity level will determine how much you need to feed him.

or she will work with you anyway. Suggest a blood test before you switch your dog to raw, and then test every six months or so to determine that balances are correct. You don't want to lose a good veterinarian over this issue, and requesting the blood tests may help to keep your veterinarian in your corner.

Talk to an animal nutritionist if you are serious about cooking for your dog. Make sure you have the freezer and refrigerator room, too. If you only have one or two Dachshunds, either standard or miniature, just the freezer that is part of your refrigerator ought to be fine, but many people who feed raw like the convenience of a larger freezer because it enables them to take advantage of sales on bones and raw foods. One veterinarian who feeds and recommends raw also recommends pounding or grinding all bones.

Keep in mind that the key to feeding bones is that they are raw and fresh! Cooked bones are bad for dogs. They are hard and brittle, and poultry bones especially can splinter and pierce a dog's

Taking a Special Diet on the Road

If you're travelling with your dog, carry a cooler, or plan to buy fresh meat as you travel. It takes a bit more effort than a commercial food, but it can be done. If you supply daily packets of your dog's food, most boarding kennels should be willing to continue your dog's raw diet. This is something to find out about ahead of time. Nobody likes surprises, so don't just show up at your boarding kennel with your raw food, and don't be disappointed if the kennel operator refuses to feed the bones. Settle everything ahead of time.

stomach or intestines. Many raw food diets suggest recreational bones for your dog to gnaw on, but it's important not to let these bones just lay around the garden for days at a time. After a day or two, these bones will dry out and become as much of a problem as cooked bones. The meat and bones you feed your Dachshund should also be organic, especially with a raw diet.

While commercial foods are certainly fast and easy, feeding raw doesn't have to take up inordinate amounts of time. For instance, you can make up enough of your vegetable mixture to last a week or two, and then freeze it in daily amounts in small containers.

VARYING YOUR DOG'S DIET

There's another school of thought that says that no matter what you feed your dog, there should be variety. Our dogs shouldn't eat the same food day in and day out. One of the reasons that a food change should be done gradually, over a week or so, is because of the habit of feeding one food constantly. If you know any vegetarians, you'll know that they get physically ill if they eat meat. That's because their system hasn't experienced meat in so long that it doesn't know how to deal with it. I've read that deer herds can starve to death in a bad winter even if food is provided, because it is not food they are used to.

Veterinarian Wendy Blount notes that, "we know that digestive

Your Dachshund will need to have a ready supply of cool, fresh water in an easy-to-clean, durable bowl.

Small pieces of peeled carrots make excellent snacks for Dachshunds.

enzymes are induced by foods found in the digestive tract. It's quite possible that dogs get diarrhoea when we change their diet just because we ruin their ability to digest a variety of foods by feeding only a single type food. If you ate only biscuits and chicken every day for three years, you'd probably be doubled over in pain if you ate an orange, which is full of wonderful nutrients. Oranges causing pain doesn't mean that oranges are bad for you—just the opposite, you should eat them more often. I have German Shepherds, a breed notorious for their sensitive GI tracts. Every time I open a new bag of dog food, it's a different brand and flavour than the last. And every night I open a tin of food that is different than the night before. They get a variety of fresh foods as a "top dressing." I have a list of several dozen varieties of kibble and tinned foods I rotate through—all whole foods with no chemical preservatives."

I can't tell you what is right or wrong for your dog. That's going to depend on your lifestyle and on what you learn from your breeder, your veterinarian and other Dachshund owners.

YOUR DOG'S DISHES

Whatever food you choose, feed your dog from a clean dish and make sure he always has access to fresh, clean water. The kind of dish is important. You want to choose something that is durable, easy to clean, and doesn't slip. Stainless steel and heavy ceramic are the best choices. However, if you decide on that adorable ceramic bowl decorated with bones, make sure the paint and glaze are lead-free.

Your Dachshund's Unique Needs

Every Dachshund is different, and it's up to you to feed your dog what he needs—neither too little nor too much.

I like a dish that is light and non-breakable, but that's just a personal preference. No matter what kind of dish you use, make sure you wash it after every meal. Just because your dog has licked the bowl clean doesn't mean it is clean. You wouldn't use your dinner dishes over and over without washing them.

If you have more than one dog, you will need to monitor them at meal times so that there's no argument over the food. Don't put the bowls down side by side, but a few feet in between should be acceptable for all. You don't want the dominant dog to get all the food, and you certainly don't want a dogfight. If eating together doesn't work with your dogs, you'll need to separate them. Feeding in separate areas, or in crates, also ensures that each dog gets whatever may be added to his food, like a supplement or medicine. When dogs are fed separately, you can tell if one is off his food, or hasn't taken his medication. If you're feeding raw, this also gives each dog a chance to really chew the bones, instead of gulping everything.

Dachshunds are always willing to eat. If you could ask your dog how often he wanted to eat, he would probably say, "Hourly!" Good thing you're in charge of feeding him! Adult dogs should be fed either once or twice a day, though most people find twice a day preferable. Puppies, of course, get four meals a day when they're first weaned off their mother's milk, then three, and, by about the age of six months, twice a day.

Another option is to free-feed your dog, which means that you put down the daily food and it's there all day, whenever your dog wants to eat it. In a multiple-dog household, this simply won't work, because one of the dogs will eat more than his share. If you only have one dog, you can try this, but with a Dachshund, chances are all the food will be gone in the first few minutes.

Other problems with free feeding are that if you are trying to give any kind of medication with the food, you'll want that

A Sample Raw Diet

To get a sense of what goes into feeding a raw diet, here is a sample daily allowance as prepared by veterinarian Jean Hofve. The amounts listed are adequate for one day's feeding of a 20- to 35-pound dog. Dachshunds should receive one-third to one-half these amounts. You should adjust the amounts of ingredients and supplements proportionally to your dog's weight. Starches may be decreased in case of digestive problems or for weight loss.

Choose one protein source (meat amounts given in raw weight):

- 1/3 pound (.15 kg) boneless chicken breast or thigh, chopped

- 3 large hard-boiled eggs, chopped

- 1/3 pound (.15 kg) lean beef, or lamb, ground or minced

- Optional: once a week, substitute 4 oz organic liver for half of any meat source

Choose one starch source:

- 2 cups (.9 kg) cooked macaroni

- 3 cups (1.4 kg) cooked potato, with skin, chopped or mashed

- 2 cups (.9 kg) cooked rice

- 2 cups (.9 kg) rolled oats, quick, cooked

Supplements:

- Pureed veggie mix, raw or steamed (up to 1 cup)

- 1 tablespoon olive oil, or 1/2 tbsp olive and 1/2 tbsp flaxseed oil

- 400 mg calcium (elemental, as calcium citrate or carbonate)

- 1/4 tsp salt substitute (potassium chloride)—give 3 or 4 times a week

- 1 multiple vitamin-mineral supplement (human quality) dose adjusted for weight

- 1 probiotic/digestive enzyme supplement

medication given at specific times; also, you won't be as aware of your dog's appetite, which is one of the first indicators that your dog is not feeling well.

HOW MUCH TO FEED

How much you feed your dog will depend on his activity level and age. Puppies will eat more than your average adult, and an active adult will eat more than the older couch potato.

Most dog foods have a recommended amount for feeding, but you'll want to talk to other Dachshund owners and adjust that amount for your Dachshund. The amount you feed also will depend on whether you have a standard or a miniature Dachshund.

Typically, standard puppies should be fed about 1/2 cup of kibble with a teaspoon of tinned food four times a day. Reduce that to three feedings a day at about 16 weeks of age, then cut back to two feedings a day by four months. Miniature Dachshunds will need about half that amount.

If you feed raw, the recommended amount of raw meaty bones is two to three percent of your dog's body weight. Dogs on the BARF diet are fed twice daily because the morning meal is always the raw, meaty bones, and the evening meal is a vegetable mix, with muscle or organ meat.

AGE-APPROPRIATE FEEDING

You'll want to feed your puppy a premium puppy food for his first few months, switching to an adult food when he is about six months old. If you plan to feed raw, you might want to pound or grind the bones until your Dachshund is an adult.

Adult dog foods come with varying levels of protein and fat, but all are geared for an active, healthy adult. If you're doing a lot of activities with your dog, you may want a food with a higher level of protein. Talk to your breeder about this, as well as your veterinarian.

Senior dogs (those seven to eight years old or older) start to slow down, just like people. They may not want to walk as far, and they tend to take more naps. It may be that the food that has kept your Dachshund healthy all these years is now too rich, or isn't being digested as well. You should consider feeding a senior formula, which has a lower level of protein and may contain beneficial supplements like glucosamine and chondroitin for stiffening joints, or other vitamins/minerals, foods, or herbs.

With their typically hearty appetites, pleading eyes, and love of naps, it's easy for Dachshunds to pack on the pounds. Keep an eye on your dog's weight and manage it accordingly.

Getting your Dachshund out for more frequent walks or visits with other dogs can help him get back in shape.

DON'T LET YOUR DACHSHUND GET FAT

No matter what kind of food you give your Dachshund, obesity can be a problem. Dachshunds love to eat, and they are very good at persuading you that they are starving. It's so hard to resist those big brown eyes and that cute face. For your dog's health, however, you must resist. That doesn't mean you can't ever give him a bit of your scrambled egg or a piece of cheese or a nibble of your pizza crust. It does mean that you can't give him treats and goodies constantly.

Factor the amount and types of treats you give with what your dog is fed as his regular food. For instance, if you are having a training session every day—especially if you are using clicker training—you will be giving your dog a lot of treats. Cut those treats up into very small pieces, and subtract a bit of kibble or a teaspoon or so of the tinned food to compensate.

Is My Dachshund Obese?

To gauge your dog's weight, look at him from the top. He should have a bit of an indentation behind the ribs. Feel your Dachshund's sides. You should be able to feel the ribs. If you can't feel the ribs, your Dachshund needs to go on a diet.

If you have eggs every morning and you and your Dachshund both enjoy sharing, think about that when you are feeding your dog his regular meal. My dogs get a dog biscuit at night, as well as a smaller one when I leave the house and they stay behind. Some people always give their dog a biscuit when the dog comes in from the garden. When I add cheese to my lunchtime sandwich, both dogs get a bite of cheese. Part of the fun of having a dog is getting to sneak them a sliver of turkey or watching them catch popcorn in mid-air.

Sometimes we forget how small our dogs really are and how

quickly they can gain weight. Two or three pounds (kg) doesn't sound like much to an adult human, but for a Dachshund, that can mean the difference between ideal weight and overweight. A fat dog is not attractive, but more than that, he is not healthy. Extra pounds on your Dachshund can lead to heart problems, breathing problems, and diabetes. It can also add stress to the back and joints, and that can lead to arthritis, a painful and debilitating condition.

Taking weight off a dog is so much easier than a person. Dogs can't raid the refrigerator in the middle of the night, or reach for a second helping. If your dog is overweight, cut back on treats. This may be enough, but if not, reduce the amount of food at each meal. Try increasing your dog's exercise. Maybe an extra walk down the road will do the trick, or a little more playtime. A good game of hide-and-seek in the house can help burn some calories, and you and your dog will love it.

So many times we equate love with food treats. Our dogs ask for so little and they love goodies so much. Be sensible with treats. Don't kill your dog with kindness.

Being Smart About Treats

There are two main things to remember when offering treats: First, no more than 10 percent of your dog's total amount of food should be "people food" or treats. Second, make sure that the treats

Foods to Avoid

Foods to be careful of include grapes, raisins, onions, and macadamia nuts. Don't panic if your dog eats a couple of raisins or a grape, or a piece of onion if you accidentally drop one. If your dog finds an entire box of raisins, though, and thinks it is a wonderful snack, check in with your veterinarian. Too many Macadamia nuts can cause temporary paralysis, so be careful your Dachshund can't reach that tempting bowl of nibbles.

Your little Dachshund can become overweight easily if you give in to his charm and overfeed him.

Who could resist this face? Regardless of how cute he is, don't feed your Dachshund from your table, and ask him to stay or wait before he gets his meals or treats.

Pupsicles

Most dogs love the occasional ice cube, especially on a hot day. For an added treat, you can make what a friend of mine calls "pupsicles." Just take a tin of low salt chicken or beef stock, or mix a dry bouillon cube with water according to the directions. Add an additional tin of water to the stock. Put the stock in ice cube trays and freeze.

are appropriate. Treats marketed especially for dogs are fine, and many people foods are okay in small amounts. Others may cause tummy upsets. For instance, at Christmas, a bit of turkey is fine, but stay away from the stuffing, or excessive gravy, which could be too rich. When you're making pies, a spoonful of the filling won't hurt, but don't give your Dachshund bites of the finished pie.

Stay away from all chocolates. The theobromine in chocolate can be fatal to dogs, and even if it doesn't kill your dog, it can make him sick. The American Animal Hospital Association (AAHA) offers these figures for fatal doses of chocolate: Ten ounces of milk chocolate, or 1/2 to 1 ounce of baking chocolate can kill a small dog; 1 to 1 1/2 pounds of milk chocolate or 2 to 3 ounces of baking chocolate can kill a medium-sized dog.

Liver Treats

People who show their dogs use liver treats as bait to get their dogs to look alert and happy. Whether you show your dog or not, liver makes a wonderful treat. The fast way to make the treats is to put the liver in the microwave, cover it with a paper towel, and microwave for three minutes on high. Turn the pieces over, and cook it again for three more minutes on high. The result is a piece of cooked liver that looks a lot like shoe leather. Not attractive to you, but your Dachshund will love it! Feed tiny pieces as a reward.

Another recipe is to put the liver in cold water. Rinse. Add the rinsed liver to a pan of cold water and bring it to a boil. Boil for 20 minutes. Put the liver on a baking sheet, sprinkle with garlic powder, and bake for 20 to 30 minutes at 150 degrees centigrade. This, too, will come out looking shrivelled and unappetizing to you—but not to your dog! Keep extra in the freezer.

TEACHING GOOD FOOD MANNERS

Teach good food manners from the time your Dachshund is a

Don't Let Him Beg

I have always made it a house rule to never, ever feed the dogs from the table, so we don't have much trouble there. If you don't mind the thought of a begging dog sitting by your chair drooling for the next 14 to 16 years, fine, but really, you'll be happier if that habit doesn't start.

puppy. Puppies are so cute it's hard to imagine that we might not want them to be constant beggars when they reach adulthood. Also, what might be manageable when you have just one Dachshund may be annoying if you have two or three or four.

When we got our first dog, I always gave her the milk that was left in my cereal bowl. When we got another dog, I had to divide that milk. With dog number three, I had to actually pour extra milk and make sure each dog got some. It wasn't as cute anymore. The same thing happened with evening snacks.

Dogs love popcorn, and plain popcorn is a fine treat for dogs. But sharing with one dog is far different from sharing with three or four. When we had four dogs, whenever my husband made popcorn, all four would sit and stare until they got their share. Even with only two dogs now, they still demand their popcorn.

To Get, You Have to Give

Right from the beginning, you can use feeding time as a perfect way to get in some training. Start by asking your dog to sit before you put down the bowl of food. Just hold the bowl slightly above and over your dog's head and say, "Sit." As he follows the bowl with

his eyes, he should sink into a sit. Immediately praise him and put down the bowl. When he's learned to sit, start teaching him to stay.

Give the sit command, and then place the palm of your hand in front of his face and say, "Stay" or "Wait." Put the food dish down and immediately say, "Okay," or whatever release word you choose. Gradually increase the time until your Dachshund is waiting for you to release him before he starts to eat.

Teaching your Dachshund with food can make the entire process a game, since Dachshunds are always interested in doing whatever will get them the food! If you decide to try clicker training, you'll find that your Dachshund catches on very quickly to the idea of rewards. (More about that in Chapter 6.)

While your puppy is small, teach him that you are allowed to take things away from him and he must not resist or growl or snap. Put the food dish down and wait until your dog starts eating. Pick up the dish, add something tasty, and give the food back. This is letting him know that if you take it away, he'll get something even better. You can do the same thing if he's playing with a toy. Trade him the toy for a biscuit.

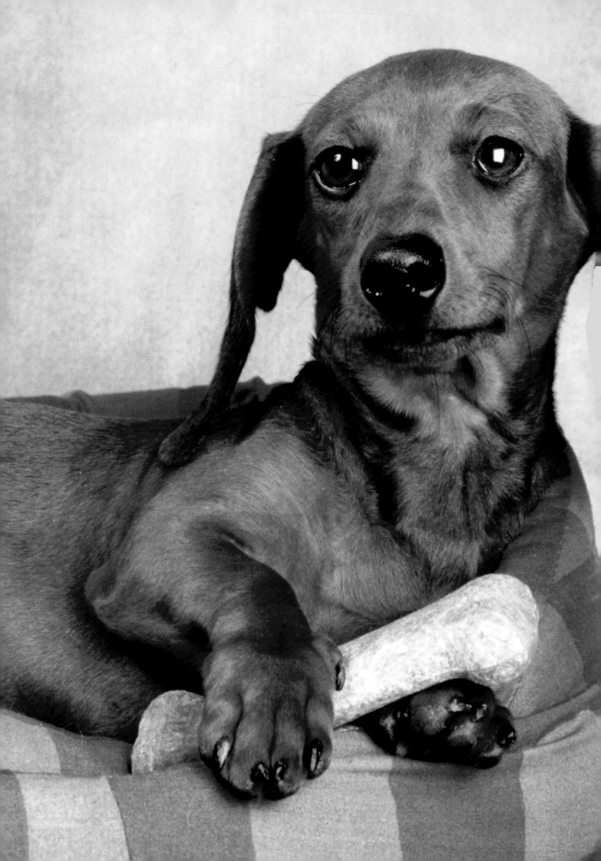

Chapter

5

GROOMING

Your Dachshund

chapter on grooming your Dachshund needs three different approaches, depending on which coat type your Dachshund has. Let's start with some grooming basics and then discuss each coat type.

GROOMING BASICS

Besides helping to keep your dog and your house tidy, grooming is a good time to check your Dachshund for any injuries or problems. Running your hands over your Dachshund and feeling his legs and feet on a regular basis can help you spot problems while they're still small. You can detect skin problems, any lumps or bumps, or signs of a flea or tick invasion. While you're checking your dog over, you also can slide a hand over his ribs. If you can't feel them, it may be time for a doggy diet.

Check your Dachshund's eyes for any discharge or cloudiness. Open his mouth just to make sure all is clear. How are your Dachshund's ears? Any dog with a folded ear can develop ear infections. Catch them early with your grooming once-over. Also, run your hands around your Dachshund's neck and check for swollen lymph glands.

Grooming Tables

With small dogs like Dachshunds, the grooming process is greatly simplified with a grooming table. You can buy them at pet supply stores or through pet catalogues. I wouldn't be without my grooming table. I bought it originally because I was showing my dogs, but even if I weren't, I would really appreciate the table. It puts the dog up on my level and saves both my back and my knees. Also, my dogs are less apt to scoot away from me when they're up on the table. That's not to say they will stay there without help. Use a grooming noose, or keep a firm hold of your dog if you put him on a table. Dachshunds are too small to launch themselves from a table without getting hurt, but that doesn't mean they won't try.

Some people prefer to brush their dogs while they're relaxing and watching television. If that works for you, just leave your brush by your favourite chair, wear old clothes, or cover your lap with a towel, and brush away.

The process and routine of grooming a small dog like a Dachshund are simplified when you use a grooming table.

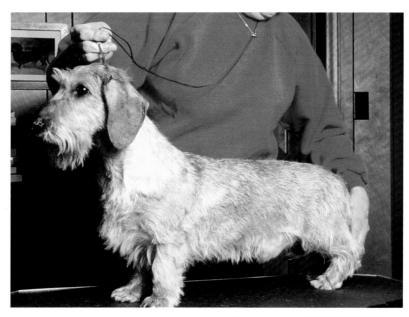

ALL DOGS NEED GROOMING

If you have a Smooth Dachshund, you may feel that your dog, as a shorthaired dog, will not require much in the way of grooming at all. It is true that Smooth Dachshunds don't have a labour-intensive coat. That short, sleek coat won't mat or get tangles or hold a lot of mud or dirt, but that doesn't mean that a Dachshund doesn't need to be groomed. Don't be fooled by that neat look. Dachshunds shed, and you need to groom them to get rid of dead hair and keep them looking and feeling their best. When your Dachshund is shedding, you'll want to brush him at least every other day to prevent all those tiny little hairs from covering everything in your home. Even when your Dachshund isn't actively shedding, a good weekly brushing will help keep things under control.

Brushing a Smooth

With either a Smooth or a Longhair, brushing is the key to getting all that hair off your Dachshund before it comes off on your sofa. Use a soft bristle brush or a slicker brush on your Smooth and, for loosening the coat when your Smooth is shedding, invest in a rubber curry comb. You can follow the grain of the coat from neck to tail, and it will loosen all the dead fur.

Brushing a Longhair

With a Longhair, pay attention to behind the ears and elbows, as

The Benefits of Good Grooming

Any disease, soreness, or problem of any kind is much easier to treat if it's caught early, and doing a hands-on survey of your Dachshund while you're grooming is a good way to make that early catch.

Grooming Table Substitutes

If you don't want to invest in a grooming table, you can use a rubber mat on top of almost any surface. I once used my clothes dryer, and I know people who use the kitchen counter. Outdoors, a picnic table also makes a good grooming area. Just make sure that you cover slippery surfaces with a non-slip mat. Even a rubber bath mat will work. You want your Dachshund to feel secure and safe while you're making him look his best.

those areas are usually the first to mat. Comb out that hair, gently working out any snarls or knots with your fingers. If you have a Longhair, eventually his "shawl," the longer hair around his neck, will need to be thinned from time to time, or he will start to look like a lion. It's probably best to have a groomer take care of this.

Brushing a Wirehair

If you have a Wirehair, the grooming is a bit different. Many pet owners use clippers or have a groomer clip the dog. This is faster

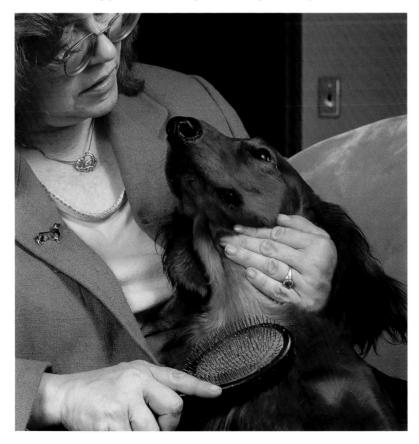

Some people prefer to brush their dogs while they're sitting down and relaxing.

For Smooth and Longhaired Dachshunds, a soft bristle or slicker brush will loosen and remove the dead fur. Work from the head to the tail.

and easier than stripping, but softens the dog's coat. If you ever plan to show your Wirehair, never, ever use clippers. If you have the time, you can learn to hand-strip your Wirehair, which is a way of plucking out all the dead hair, clearing the way for new growth. Some people also use special stripping knives. Talk to your breeder or a groomer about learning to do this.

TRIMMING NAILS

Next come the nails. If you've just given your dog a bath, then that's a good time to trim his nails, because the water will have softened them up a bit. But if you're just doing a general grooming session that doesn't include a bath, you've still got to do the nails as well. Dog nails grow at different rates, and if you

Grooming Time as Bonding Time

Don't think of grooming as just a chore to get through as quickly as possible. Grooming is also a good way to bond with your dog. While you're grooming, you are gently restraining your dog, preventing him from hurting either himself or you. This is teaching him in a calm way that you are the boss, the pack leader. Dogs need a leader, and once your Dachshund recognises you in that role, he's going to be a happier, calmer dog.

Grooming is a wonderful way to sneak in some training, too. Keep those treats handy and reward your Dachshund for standing still, for lifting a paw, or even lying quietly on his side, although it's hard to imagine a Dachshund lying quietly unless he's asleep!

If you have more than one dog, grooming time provides some one-on-one time for each dog. There's no competition, no race to see who gets into your lap first. It's just you and one dog, enjoying each other.

walk your dog regularly on pavement, that may be enough to keep the nails worn down. However, sooner or later, you will have to cut your dog's nails. Dachshunds are notorious for not liking this process, so you may need help.

Dachshunds are small, but that compact little body is muscular. If you are fortunate enough to have a helper, have them sit in a chair and hold the Dachshund on his back, with the dog's head under the helper's chin. Have them hold on gently but firmly. Take your clippers in one hand and your Dachshund's paw in the other. Again, use a gentle but very firm grip. You don't want your dog pulling away when you are cutting.

Cut the tip of the nail, and try to avoid hitting the quick. The quick is the dark vein running down the middle of the nail. If your Dachshund has black nails, which is likely, this can be tricky. Better to trim just a little at a time than to hit the quick. If you do hit the quick, don't panic. Use a bit of styptic powder to stop the bleeding, give your Dachshund a treat, and continue.

Grinding Nails

Another way to trim your Dachshund's nails is to use a grinding tool. My dogs much prefer this to clipping. Start getting your puppy used to the tool by turning it on and gently holding a paw on the tool so he can feel the vibration. Give him a treat. Turn the tool off. After a few days of holding paws against the tool, grasp a paw firmly and grind a nail. Try to do all the nails on one foot, but if your Dachshund starts to fight you, stop for the day and try

Getting Professional Help

A third alternative is to find a groomer you like and have her do the nails. I always do that with my male. It may be a coward's way out, but it's better than having nails that could deform your Dachshund's foot and make walking a slippery or painful affair.

Wirehaired Dachshunds are hand-stripped by professional groomers. Wires also need particular attention paid to their eyebrows and beards.

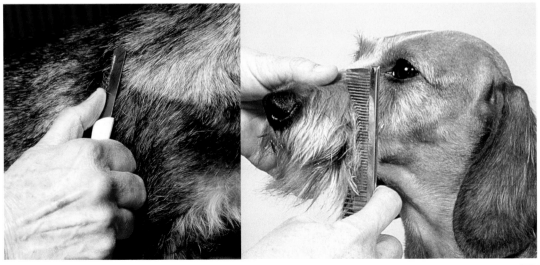

Once your dog learns that having his nails clipped is relatively painless and earns him treats, he won't mind the procedure.

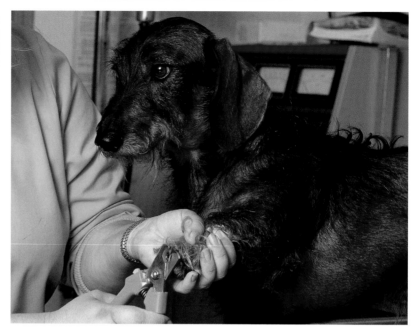

Removing Sticky Stuff

If your Dachshund gets something sticky in his coat, like gum, tree sap, or road tar, use an ice cube to freeze it. If the substance is brittle, it will come out of the coat more easily. Or, try peanut butter on the gooey stuff. I like both these ideas for anything on the face.

If there's something sticky on the body, hairspray soaked onto the spot may work, or try a cotton ball soaked with nail polish remover. Just be careful with both of these products, as they may irritate your Dachshund's skin.

again the next day. It shouldn't take long before your dog accepts the grinder. With one of my dogs, I still just do one foot, then stop, give a treat and a hug, then do the next foot, and so on.

MINDING THE EARS

Check your Dachshund's ears on a regular basis. Doing so helps you catch any problems while they're still small. The inside of the ear should be pink, not red. You can find special ear cleaner at pet supply shops and at most veterinarian's surgeries. Check the label to see if the product contains alcohol, which can dry out and irritate your Dachshund's ears and make them itch. Squirt some cleaner on a cotton ball, and gently clean the inside flap of your dog's ears. Also, gently clean around the outer ear. Don't ever poke into the ear canal. If you feel some deep cleaning is needed, or that your Dachshund might have a serious infection or ear mites, make an appointment with your veterinarian.

BATH TIME

Preparation Is Key

If it's time for a bath, get everything ready before you get your dog. There's no way he's going to wait patiently in one spot while you scurry around looking for your supplies. In fact, you may want to get

This Dachshund's nails are short and neat.

a small bucket and keep all the equipment for bathing in one spot.

First, think about where you're going to bathe your Dachshund. If you have a miniature, your kitchen sink may work, if you don't mind the thought of washing your dog there. If you have utility room with a large sink, that might work as well. Both of these places have the advantage over your bath of being at worktop height. This will save both your back and your knees. If your kitchen tap has a spray attachment, this is even better.

If you don't want to use a sink, then it will have to be the bath. You can buy a shower-like attachment for the bath tap, which will

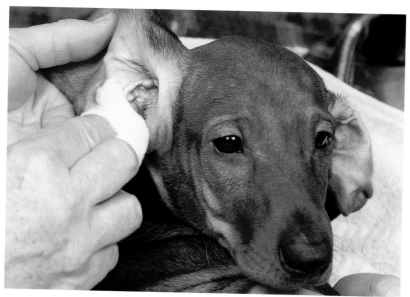

All Dachshunds need to have the insides of their ears cleaned regularly.

Shampooing Your Dog

It's best not to use shampoo formulated for people; a special dog shampoo will have the right pH balance for your dog and won't dry or irritate his skin.

make wetting down your dog and rinsing him much easier, or you can use a jug to pour water over your Dachshund. I like spray or shower attachments because I think the water gets right down to the skin and I know that all the soap residue has been removed.

Wherever you choose to give the bath, make sure there's a nonslip surface for your Dachshund. If your dog doesn't feel secure, he's more likely to struggle and more likely to injure himself. If you've selected the bath, get yourself a foam pad or a thick towel to kneel on. Get lots of towels for your dog. Change into clothing that you don't care about; something that can get soaking wet, because you will get wet, especially if your Dachshund decides to shake—and believe me, he will.

If you'd like to use a vinegar rinse, have that ready as well. Apple cider vinegar helps clear any soap residue from the coat and smells nice. For Dachshunds, use about 1/4 cup to every 4 cups of water. Be very careful not to get any soap or vinegar in your Dachshund's eyes. Some groomers add a drop of mineral oil to the eyes to help protect against soap, but others feel this just helps spread the soap. I've never used anything in my dog's eyes, but I am careful with soap. I never shampoo my dog's face. I just gently wipe the face with a damp cloth.

Some people put a cotton ball in each of the dog's ears to prevent soap and water from getting in. It's been my experience that the dog will keep shaking his head until the cotton comes out, so I never bother with the cotton, I just use care. Generally, I just clean the face and ears separately and shampoo from the head back.

If you are going to clean ears at this time, make sure you've got those cleaning supplies at hand, as well as your shampoo and towels. Once you've got your dog, close the door to the room where you're giving the bath. If you have more than one dog, they're going to be a distraction otherwise, and if you're giving the bath in the bathroom and your Dachshund manages to escape from the bath, you don't want water and suds all over the house.

It's Bath Time!

With supplies at hand and your dog in the room, you're ready to bathe. Before I put my dog in a bath or sink, I run the water and get it to the right temperature. I don't want to have to hold a squirming dog and try to adjust the water, and I don't want to risk the water being too hot. So, adjust the water, and then put the dog

in the bath. Wet the dog thoroughly with either a sprayer or with a container. Add some shampoo and work up a lather. The first application may not suds up much, but that's okay; it is cutting the dirt and oil. Rinse, then lather again. Don't neglect the feet. Rinse again, and keep rinsing until the water runs clear. Make sure you get all the soap off. Pay attention to the area behind the elbows and on the stomach, and remember to rinse those tootsies!

Try to wrap a towel around your dog before he comes out of the bath. Always lift the dog out; don't let him try to scramble out on his own. He could easily get hurt. Towel your dog as dry as possible. This will take more than one towel, so be prepared. In warm weather, this may be enough. If you want to use a hair dryer on your Longhair, either use a special dog hair dryer, or, if you're using your own dryer, put it on its lowest setting. Dogs are very sensitive, and a setting that is fine for a human is too hot for a dog. If your dryer has an air-only setting, that's even better.

If you're doing the bath at home, don't let your dog outside immediately following the bath. Nine times out of ten a dog will roll in the grass, or worse, the nearest patch of dirt. After all your hard work, enjoy it awhile before you let your dog get dirty again.

Recipe For Relief

A cup of oatmeal and a cup of baking soda mixed into two pints of warm water can make a soothing rinse if your Dachshund is suffering from any kind of dermatitis.

With all your supplies at hand, adjust the water temperature and then put your Dachshund in the bath.

Be sure to have clean, dry towels at the ready so you can rub down and dry off your Dachshund after his bath.

CARING FOR YOUR DOG'S TEETH

Dachshund puppies are like all puppies everywhere: they love to chew. Chewing feels good when puppies are teething, and, depending on what they chew, it also helps keep their teeth clean and their gums healthy. Chewing is also one of the ways puppies learn about their world. Human toddlers and puppies are alike in that they will try to put anything and everything into their mouths.

Appropriate Chew Toys

It's your job to make sure that what they chew on is safe. Also, if you don't want your chair rungs destroyed, or holes in your rug, or your kitchen linoleum pulled up, you should supply your puppy with approved chew toys.

If your puppy is teething, cold things will feel good on his sore gums. Wet a washcloth (one you are willing to sacrifice to sharp teeth), put it in a plastic bag, and freeze it. When it's frozen, take it out of the bag and let your puppy chew on it. An ice cube may also make a good teething toy. Keeping nylon bones in the freezer in between chewing sessions will make them more attractive, too. Raw carrots and whole apples make good, safe chew toys as well.

Hard, crunchy dog biscuits are helpful, as are nylon bones and rawhide bones or strips.

Rinse Thoroughly

Make sure you rinse your Dachshund repeatedly to remove all the soapy residue from the shampoo.

Nylon vs. Rawhide

Nylon bones get rough ends as they are chewed, acting like a toothbrush, and any small bits of nylon that may be ingested pass harmlessly through the system. Rawhide bones are also good, but require more supervision. Some dogs experience no trouble with rawhide, but other dogs tend to chew off large chunks and swallow them whole. These swallowed chunks can lead to intestinal blockage or stomach upset. Rawhide strips are more likely to cause this kind of a problem than a rawhide bone, but both can be dangerous. The rawhide form least likely to lead to trouble is the pressed rawhide bone, which is made of tiny shavings of rawhide that are moulded into a bone shape. This eliminates the worry of the dog biting off and swallowing large, indigestible chunks.

Hard nylon bones make excellent chews for Dachshunds. The nubs on this one also stimulate the gums.

Rawhide doesn't last as long as nylon bones, either. While a nylon bone may seem more expensive, it will be cheaper in the long run. Even small dogs like Dachshunds can demolish large rawhide bones quickly. Also, if you have more than one dog, they are more apt to get into a fight over the rawhide than they are over the nylon bones.

Bones

Real bones require the most supervision of all. While a large knucklebone is probably safe for your Dachshund to chew on, many bones can splinter or develop sharp points that can harm your dog. Swallowing bone shards can lead to serious problems if those pieces should pierce the intestines. Even with smooth bones, such as beef marrow bones, if your dog is an aggressive chewer, he can end up with a large mass of indigestible bone in his stomach, which can lead to vomiting, or even a blockage in the intestine. Real bones, if

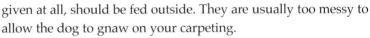

given at all, should be fed outside. They are usually too messy to allow the dog to gnaw on your carpeting.

Rope toys can be very effective at cleaning your dog's teeth, but again, supervise your dog while he plays with this kind of a toy. Dachshunds, even puppies, can totally destroy a toy in very little time, and you don't want your dog to swallow the strings, which could cause serious intestinal damage.

(Carefully) Give a Dog a Bone

If you do give your Dachshund a real bone to enjoy in the garden, make sure that you discard it after a day or two. Any longer than that and it will get dry and hard and can cause as much damage as a cooked bone.

Brushing the Teeth

Besides providing appropriate chew toys for your dog, you also can help with his dental health by brushing his teeth regularly. Dental care is as important in dogs as it is in people, and starting young will help to protect your dog's health. Although dogs are not as susceptible to tooth decay as humans, they do develop plaque, which, if not removed, hardens to tartar. Tartar, in turn, can

There are toothbrushes and toothpaste made specially for dogs, making proper oral hygiene easier than ever.

cause abscesses, and the bacteria from those abscesses can circulate in the system and lead to pneumonia or heart, liver, or kidney problems.

There are special brushes for brushing your dog's teeth, as well as smaller plastic "brushes" that fit over your finger. Or, you can wrap a piece of gauze around your finger and use that to go over the dog's teeth and gently rub the gums. Most veterinarians and pet supply stores also have special pastes for brushing your dog's teeth. These pastes come in flavours like chicken or liver. If you use a paste, make sure it is a paste made especially for dogs; never use human toothpaste on your dog.

Bad Breath

Your dog's breath will never smell like a bouquet of spring flowers, but it shouldn't make you gag, either. If you notice that

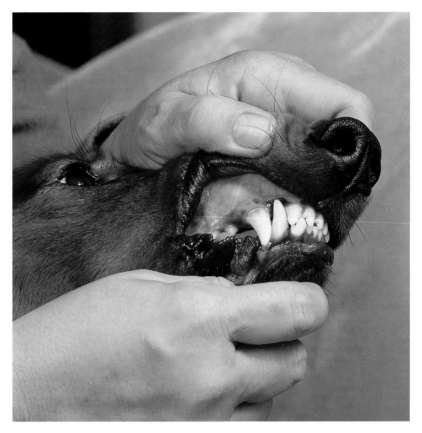

Did You Know?

Dental care is easily overlooked, but statistics show that 75 percent of all dogs have some kind of periodontal problem by the time they are four years old. Include your Dachshund's mouth and teeth in every health check.

your Dachshund's breath is really bad, check out his mouth. Make sure there are no chunks of food or bone stuck anywhere. Take a look at his teeth at the same time: Are they clean, or covered with plaque?

If you think the cause of the odour is just temporary because of something your dog may have eaten, a few chlorophyll tablets might be just the thing, or try giving your dog a rawhide, nylon, or real bone to chew to help scrape off some of the plaque. The occasional piece of raw carrot will help do the same thing.

If you're brushing your Dachshund's teeth regularly, but there's still bad breath, it may be time for a professional cleaning.

When you're at your veterinarian's surgery for the cleaning, ask for recommendations to prevent bad breath. Your veterinarian may suggest switching from a soft food to a hard kibble. He may want to schedule your Dachshund for regular cleanings. Not all dogs need frequent cleanings, but some do.

Whatever you think may be the cause of doggy bad breath, don't ignore it. Bad breath may be an indication of something more serious. Instead of just trying to avoid your dog's breath, see if you can identify any particular smell. A sweet, fruity smell could mean your dog has diabetes, especially if he is drinking or urinating more than usual and is losing weight. If his breath smells like urine, he might have a kidney disease. A foul odour that's accompanied by vomiting, loss of appetite, swelling of the abdomen, or yellowing of the eyes or gums could indicate a liver disorder.

Professional Cleanings

Your veterinarian may at some time in your dog's life recommend a professional cleaning for your dog's teeth. This involves anaesthetising your dog. While your dog is asleep, the veterinarian or technician removes any tartar buildup, then cleans and polishes your dog's teeth, much like your dentist cleans your own teeth. If any cracked or broken teeth are found, they will be removed at the same time. If there are any abscesses, or if there is infection anywhere in the gum, your dog will probably be put on an antibiotic.

If your dog is older, the veterinarian also may recommend blood tests before the cleaning to make sure the dog can safely handle the anaesthesia. This safeguard is well worth it, and, with older dogs, may help your veterinarian detect other health problems as well.

Not all dogs are alike, of course. Some dogs may need their teeth cleaned every six months; others may go their entire lives without needing a professional cleaning. Have your veterinarian check your dog's teeth at least once a year, and if you notice that your Dachshund's breath smells more than his normal "dog breath," or if he is drooling, pawing at his mouth, or having trouble eating hard food and no longer wants to chew on toys or bones, make an appointment with your veterinarian.

TRAINING AND BEHAVIOUR
of Your Dachshund

Many people think small dogs don't need any training, and it's true that small dogs can be easily scooped up if they're getting into trouble. Even a standard Dachshund can be picked up with a bit of effort, but you and your Dachshund will both be happier if he has some training. Your Dachshund will know there are limits, and he will respect you as the one who has set those limits.

All dogs, even small dogs, are pack animals. They are social and need to be part of a group, or a pack. Just two dogs can be a pack. Or, your dog's pack may be you and your family. Every pack needs a leader, and if there is no leader, your dog will try to fill the position. He may not even really want to be the leader, but someone needs to lead, and he'll feel he has to do it if no one else does.

ARE YOU A FAIR LEADER?

Even with a small dog, you need to be the leader of the pack. You do this by being firm, fair, and consistent. You don't do it by yelling or screaming. You set the rules, not the dog. This doesn't mean that you don't have lots of cuddle time and together time, but it does mean that you pick those times. Even small dogs can be possessive. It's just fine to allow your Dachshund to join you on the couch or on your bed, but make it at your invitation, not whenever he feels like it. Decide on a command. It doesn't have to be fancy. Most likely, just patting the seat or the bed beside you will be enough of an invitation. After awhile, tell him, "Off," and help him to the floor. If your bed or couch is high, helping him is always a good idea so your Dachshund doesn't hurt himself. You might even want to make a ramp or a small set of stairs.

WHAT DO YOU WANT YOUR DACHSHUND TO DO?

There are two levels of training—household manners and formal

Taking the Lead

It's important that your dog understands that you make the decisions. You don't want to head for your favourite easy chair and find a Dachshund happily curled up and ready to challenge you for the right to sit there. It's not likely that your Dachshund will ever challenge you, but all dogs have that potential.

training. Even if you have no interest in formal training, all dogs should exhibit good household manners. Household manners can vary with the household, but housetraining is pretty basic. Other "manners" training might include not jumping on the furniture, no begging at the table, no jumping up on people, and no excessive barking. You also might want to teach your Dachshund to leave the cat or some other household pet alone.

Establishing Rules

Waiting to be fed, and not charging out the door ahead of you when you're going for a walk are two more examples of household manners. Again, you are the pack leader. The leader always goes first. Make your Dachshund sit at the door on your way for a walk. Step through the door first, then call your dog through. Do this when feeding, as well. Have your Dachshund wait until you put the food dish down. Take the dish away occasionally, and then give it back. You are the leader and should be able to do this at any time.

If your Dachshund doesn't understand what you want him to do while training, it will be hard for him to comply.

In fact, all the human members of your family should be above your Dachshund in pack rank. Your Dachshund will learn quickly what he should and shouldn't do as long as you are consistent and patient. Part of the consistency means that the entire family must be part of the training team. It does no good for Mom to try to teach the dog not to jump up if Dad and the kids encourage the dog to jump up, or if they pet and praise him when he does. That's sending a mixed message.

The same goes for housetraining. I once heard about a puppy who was taking a long time to understand the concept of going outdoors. Finally, someone in the family realised that, with all the different doors and sliding doors in their house, family members were going in and out whichever door was handiest. The puppy never got a sense of which door he should go to when he needed to go out, and there was no designated area outside that was his spot. Once everyone agreed on one door and one area of the garden, the puppy quickly learned the routine.

Every human family member should be established as higher in the "pack" hierarchy than your dog.

Right from the beginning, agree on what will be allowed and what won't. There's nothing nicer than snuggling with your Dachshund on the couch, but if the family rule is no dogs on the furniture, then make sure no one allows the dog on the couch, ever, not even as a cute little puppy. The same goes for sleeping on beds. And, if you don't want your little chowhound looking pathetic and begging for some popcorn every time you have a snack, then don't feed him a handful while you're watching a DVD. Ever.

In the wild, predators develop habits that help them to find food in the most efficient way possible. If a wolf catches a rabbit in a particular spot, he's likely to continue to visit that spot, as this may be a regular path for rabbits.

Preventing Bad Habits

It's a lot harder to break a dog of a habit like begging than it is to start the habit, so think carefully about what you will and will not accept, and make sure everyone in the family knows and follows the rules.

SOCIALISING YOUR DACHSHUND

Dachshunds are by nature friendly and loving, but it's up to you to encourage those traits. A puppy raised in isolation may be shy and fearful. Socialisation is an important part of your commitment

With people you trust or in a class situation, it's great to be able to let your Dachshund socialise with other dogs.

Helping Your Dachshund Make Friends

If there are no dog parks and no neighbourhood dogs that are good candidates as playmates, consider enrolling in a puppy kindergarten class or an obedience class so that your Dachshund can get used to being around other dogs.

to your dog.

Start from the day your puppy comes home. Put his crate in a part of the house that sees a lot of activity, like the kitchen or the family room. Let him get used to the sounds of dinner being prepared, the phone ringing, the kettle whistling. Let him hear the television or a radio. Have family and friends pet and play with the puppy. Introduce him to different toys and to different surfaces underfoot. Carpeting, tile, a piece of plastic, or wood—all of these things help to build confidence in your puppy.

Once your puppy has all his shots, take him for walks around the neighbourhood. Encourage people to gently pet your puppy. If you don't have children, find some. Children, with their sudden movements and high-pitched voices, may frighten a dog if he is not accustomed to them, and a frightened dog may bite. I made sure I took my male to places where there were children. I supervised

closely, but I encouraged children to pet him and play with him.

Don't let children grab your Dachshund around the middle and lift. It's not good for your Dachshund's back, and it may startle him and cause him to snap. In that position, the child's face is right next to the dog's muzzle. Children should be encouraged to pet your dog, but never to tightly hug or lift your dog.

Besides neighbourhood children, I took my dog to Girl Scout meetings. While teaching the scouts how to approach a strange dog, how to pet a dog, and how to give a dog a treat, I was also teaching my dog that strangers were nothing to be afraid of and might even have goodies.

Take your Dachshund with you when you run errands. Carry him into the bank. Sit on a bench at a shopping centre. Dachshunds are so cute that people are going to want to pet your dog. Let them. Carry extra treats and ask some of the people to give the treats to your dog.

If there are mostly women in your house or in your circle of friends, make an effort to find men to pet and play with your Dachshund. Find big men with beards. Find people wearing hats and glasses. Take your Dachshund to a playground and let him see bicycles and skateboards. If there's a dog park in your neighbourhood, even if you don't feel you can let your dog loose in the park, visit the park and get your Dachshund used to seeing other dogs. If you have a friend or neighbour with a friendly dog, introduce the dogs.

If the dog is much bigger than your Dachshund, be careful. A big dog could accidentally hurt your Dachshund in play, or your Dachshund could feel threatened by a larger dog looming over him and he could snap or bite. It's good for your dog to have other dogs as friends, but make the introductions slowly, on neutral

Crating for Parties

With my dogs, I always crate them before a party. For one thing, with the door opening and closing, I don't want to risk the dogs darting out and getting lost. For another, Dachshunds are low to the ground and might easily be stepped on by guests, or might trip a guest. Also, with so many strangers around, the dogs can get stressed. Putting them in their crates means they feel safe and secure. And, although it's hard to believe, not everyone will love your dog, especially a guest dressed up in party attire. Sure, you love your dog, but you want your guests to feel comfortable and enjoy your hospitality, and really, it won't hurt your dog to be crated for a few hours. At the end of the evening, if the dog lovers have stayed behind, you can always let your dog out for a meet and greet — and to have one or two tiny morsels of cheese.

ground, and keep the dogs on lead at all times.

Expose your dog to as many different sights and sounds as you can when he is young, and you should end up with a happy, outgoing, friendly dog.

A CRATE CAN BE GREAT

Along with your puppy's health record, a supply of food, and a toy or two, your breeder also may have talked to you about a crate for your puppy. A crate, like any tool, can be abused; however, when used correctly, it can make day-to-day living with your Dachshund much more pleasant for everyone. If your puppy came with a crate, or your breeder started crate training, then you're a step ahead. Otherwise, go get a crate now. No, it is not a cage, and no, it is not cruel. Dogs are den animals. Think of all the dogs you've seen resting under a table or a chair. They appreciate the security of a small, dark space. People see bars; dogs see security.

Crate training has multiple benefits. It not only assists in housetraining, but it provides a safe den or carrier for quiet time or travelling.

If you have a multi-dog household, or there's a lot of activity in your home, you'll find that your dog will seek out his crate on his own for an afternoon nap. If you're having a party, or the grandkids are spending the day, pop your Dachshund in his crate to keep him safe or allow him to rest.

Another good reason to have a crate for a puppy is that when you are unable to watch him, you know he will be safe. Puppies check out their world by putting everything in their mouths. That can include the fringe on your oriental rug, the rungs of the antique chair, and electrical cables. While you might be very annoyed at losing the fringe or seeing teeth marks on the chair, if your puppy chews through an electric cable, you're going to lose your puppy.

Travel is another very good reason to have a crate. For one thing, you don't want your Dachshund travelling loose in the car. A crate will keep him safe and he won't be climbing into the driver's lap and distracting him. Also, travel can be stressful. If your Dachshund has his own safe crate at the end of the trip, that will help keep him calmer. Hotels may more readily accept you and your dog if they know the dog will be crated and not left alone to chew on the bedspread. Even the best-trained dogs may have an accident due to anxiety. A crate will prevent it from ending up on the hotel room carpet.

Without a crate, your Dachshund puppy may opt to use the furniture for the frequent naps he needs.

Adjusting to the Crate

You don't want your puppy or dog to learn that whining or crying is what opens the crate door to let him out. If your dog is upset in the crate, make no noise yourself until he is quiet. The second he stops protesting, open the door and praise him. Gradually increase the amount of time in the crate.

Crate Quirks

Sometimes there will be a dog who just can't adjust to a crate, and some dogs develop their own little quirks. I've had three dogs who slept in their crates each night, but insisted that the door be left open. One dog always started out sleeping under the bed and then moved to her crate. My male won't settle down unless he's in his closed crate, but my girl prefers the freedom to roam around a bit at night. Train your dogs to accept the crate, but with time, you'll know what variations might be called for.

Your own relatives and friends also may appreciate the crate. If you're visiting and are taking the dog, a crate will reassure your loved ones that their possessions will be the same when you leave as they were when you arrived.

One of the best tools for housetraining is your crate. Dogs don't like to soil their own bed. Given a chance, and within a reasonable time frame, a puppy will learn to hold it until he is taken to an appropriate spot. The other advantage to a crate is that it has a small, easy-to-clean surface, so if the puppy does have an accident in the crate, it is easier to clean than the rug, and causes less damage (and anger).

Crate Limits

Your dog should learn to enjoy his crate, but should not be confined for more than four hours at a time.

Until your Dachshund is housetrained and about a year old, when you leave the house for work or shopping, pop him in his crate. Make sure he has water and maybe a toy or two. This does not mean put your Dachshund in a crate at 8 a.m. and leave him until you get home at 6 p.m. A crate is a useful training tool and a safe haven for

When you need to secure your dog outside for a short time (under your supervision), you may choose to use a wire exercise pen rather than a more enclosed crate.

your dog, but it is not a substitute for training, or for attention.

There is a rule for puppies is that they can be crated for their age in months, plus one. So, if your puppy is two months old, three hours is the limit. The other rule is no dog, puppy or adult, should be crated for longer than four hours at a time. If there's no family member who can give the dog a break after four hours, see if there's a neighbour who can help out, turn a utility room or bathroom into a place for your Dachshund during the day, or hire a professional pet-walking service.

There will be exceptions, of course. If you're visiting relatives and are going out for the afternoon, your adult Dachshund will not suffer if he's crated for six hours. Just make this kind of crating the exception rather than the rule. And, before you crate your Dachshund for an extended period of time, make sure he's had a chance to relieve himself.

Crate Training Your Puppy

If you have a puppy, crate training should not be difficult at all. To begin, make the crate a comfortable, enjoyable place. Put in lots of towels, a toy, and water. I like the toy to be a cuddly stuffed toy for puppies, as I think it reminds them of their littermates. Think

How to Handle Accidents

Never, ever punish your puppy for mistakes. If you catch him in the act, scoop him up with his tail between his thighs to prevent further spillage, and rush him outside. Praise him when he goes in the right place. Yelling at him after the fact does no good at all. Housetraining takes patience and observation and consistency on your part. Also, never rub your dog's nose in his mistake. This will only teach him that he needs to hide his "mistake" from you.

about a bowl that clamps to the side of the crate, or a water bottle, so the puppy won't tip the bowl over.

To introduce your puppy to the crate, allow him to investigate with the door open. Toss a small treat into the crate. When he follows, praise him. Let him come out for another small treat. Next time, toss the treat in the crate and when he goes to get it, close the door for about 30 seconds. Praise him and repeat again, this time for about 30 seconds longer. This is a great way to build his tolerance and get him used to being in his crate in a gradual way.

Most puppies readily accept the crate. Sometimes they'll cry a bit at night, especially the first two or three nights. Harden your heart, grit your teeth, and don't take him out. If you've made sure that he's relieved himself and you know he's warm and dry, just try to listen to those heart-breaking sounds without giving in. He'll get used to it, honest.

If you have more than one crate, or can easily shift your crate, let your dog sleep in the bedroom with you. It may make falling asleep a bit more difficult for those first few nights, but it will give your dog more time with you, even if you're asleep. It's like eight hours of quality time for your dog, with no effort on your part. Another advantage is that you can hear your puppy if he whines and needs to go out in the middle of the night.

Crate Training an Older Dog

If you've brought home an older dog who's never had a crate, it's still worthwhile to crate train him, but it will be more of a project. Start by putting the crate in a central place like the kitchen or family room. Leave the door open. Feed your dog in the crate, still leaving the door open. During the day, occasionally throw a tasty treat into the crate. If your dog happens to go into the crate on his own, praise and treat him. If you have a clicker, you can click and treat. After three or four days, close the door while your Dachshund is eating. Open it and let him out as soon as he's finished eating. Put a longer-lasting treat, like a rawhide or a carrot in the crate, and shut the door.

At odd times during the day, put him in the crate, shut the door, and leave him. Keep the time short, but don't ever let him out when he's barking. Wait until he is silent, and then open the door. You don't want to reward the barking. Within a couple of weeks, your dog should have accepted the crate as his den.

Crates can be fairly expensive, but they last forever, so make the investment. First you'll have to decide which kind of crate you want. For shows, or travelling, I prefer the hard-sided crates as they offer better protection. For a permanent spot at home, I like wire crates because they provide more ventilation, especially in the summer. To make it more den-like, I cover the crate with a towel. Then, in the summer, it's easy to flip the sides up to allow for more air.

It will take patience and consistency to housetrain your Dachshund.

As wonderful as crates are for training, for security, and for safety, remember that they are not a substitute for training or for companionship. If you don't have the time to spend exercising and playing and cuddling with a Dachshund, you had better think about getting a goldfish.

SUCCESSFUL HOUSETRAINING

Along with the crate training, you'll want to train your puppy

Cleaning Up the Messes

Another thing to think about is what kind of cleaning product you use to clean up after your puppy. Never use any cleaning product that contains ammonia. Puppies tend to return to whatever spot they've used before. Scent tells them they've come to the right place. Urine contains ammonia, so if you clean with an ammonia-based cleaner, that residue will tell the puppy he's in the right place. Because this is important, use a commercially prepared enzyme cleaner that removes both the stain and the odour of urine. There are many available to choose from.

The APDT

The Association of Pet Dog Trainers (APDT) certifies trainers, and its members consistently use positive-based methods. Find an APDT trainer near you through their web site, www.apdt.co.uk.

to relieve himself outdoors. Many people will tell you that Dachshunds are hard to housetrain, but part of that is based on the history of hunting dogs. Hunting dogs were selected for their ability to trail and, in the case of Dachshunds, to be fearless in the face of prey. They were not necessarily selected because they were easy to train. A Dachshund can be a bit stubborn on certain issues. Dachshunds can definitely be housetrained, but it's up to you to be consistent and to have a schedule.

There is more than one way to housetrain a puppy, but no matter what the method used, the key to success is consistency on your part, and a schedule that a young puppy can reasonably meet. No matter what method you use, when you take your puppy out, choose a word or phrase that will be your puppy's cue to "go." It could be "hurry up," or "go potty," or anything at all. Once your dog is housetrained, this phrase can come in handy. If you're going somewhere for a few hours, take your dog out, say the command phrase and your dog should relieve himself. Then you can leave him alone at home without worrying about accidents.

When you take your puppy out, take him out on a lead. You want to be able to direct him to the right spot. Puppies are fast and curious, which means they can get over and under obstacles, and they will. If you're dressed for work, you won't want to have to crawl in the dirt under a bush, and if it's 2 a.m. and you're in your nightgown, your puppy may appreciate a game of tag, but you probably won't.

Housetraining With a Crate

First, let's discuss housetraining with a crate. Take the puppy out first thing in the morning. Open the crate, remove the puppy, and head for the garden. Do not open the crate and coax the puppy to follow you through the house to the garden. The puppy is probably not going to make it that far. Carry him so that he goes in the spot you've chosen in the garden. The fewer mistakes that are made in the house, the faster the housetraining will be.

Praise your puppy when he goes in the right spot. Then take him in the house for breakfast, both his and yours. Keep him crated while you eat, just in case. Take him back out 20 to 30 minutes after he's eaten. Give him some playtime before everyone leaves for school or work, then take him out one more time. Put him back in his crate for no more than four hours. If you can't get home for lunch, see if there's a neighbour who can help. When you do get home, take the puppy out immediately. He also should be given another meal, some playtime and another trip out, and then be put back in his crate.

If you have children, this means that in another two or three hours someone will be home for another trip out and more play time. Make sure everyone understands the importance of getting the puppy outdoors when he needs to relieve himself. Puppies typically sniff and circle, but they are also very quick, and with Dachshund puppies, it's sometimes hard to tell whether they're squatting or not.

After dinner, it's out again, and another play session. Then,

There are many kinds of leads on the market that serve different purposes. Choose one that's practical and comfortable as well as stylish.

because puppies, like babies, need lots of sleep, your puppy may sleep during the evening while you're watching television. Take him out one last time at about 11 p.m. If he's kept warm all night, he should make it until you are up at 6 a.m. to start the day. Puppies are a lot like people in that regard. If your puppy gets cold in the night, he'll wake up, and if he wakes up, he'll have to go. Having a crate in the bedroom means that not only does the puppy get to be with you, but, if he wakes up and cries to go out, you'll hear him right away.

Paper Training

Suppose you have no neighbours or children and can't get away regularly for the mid-day walk. In this case, you should consider paper training. Choose a room for confining the puppy. It could be your kitchen, bathroom, or utility room. If the room is too large to easily cover the floor with newspapers, you can block off a section. Put the puppy's crate and toys and water bowl in the chosen area.

When you are home, try to follow the schedule as discussed earlier. Take the puppy out after naps, after meals, and after playtime. When unattended, place the puppy in the papered area. When you clean up, remove the top layers of paper and replace with fresh ones. After a week or so, reduce the area covered by paper. If the puppy successfully uses the paper and not the uncovered floor, reduce the area even further. Continue until all the papers have been picked up.

Puppy litter is a relatively new approach to paper training. Just like a cat, you can teach your dog to use a litter pan filled with special litter. Litter may be just the thing as an interim step, like the newspapers, or, if you live in an apartment or flat, this may be your permanent solution. Remember, whatever method you use, be patient and consistent.

Time and Patience

Housetraining may take until the puppy is 12 to 16 weeks old, or possibly longer, depending on the puppy, but it's not something that can be rushed. Also, even if your puppy seems reliable at 16 weeks, there may be lapses. If someone is home with the puppy, he can probably have the run of the house, but if you're going out, don't leave the puppy loose. Take the precaution of putting him in his crate or in a

safe room. Besides the possibility of an accident, puppies love to chew. Don't give him the chance to chew the fringe of the Oriental rug, the rung of a chair, or worse yet, an electrical cable.

Trainers and owners of today recognise that positive, reward-based training methods are the most effective and pleasant.

LEAD TRAINING

The next thing you want to think about after housetraining, or even as part of housetraining, is lead training. You may not care about having your Dachshund in a perfect heel position, but it's a good idea to teach him to walk on a lead. Even with a fenced garden, you may want to show off your darling with a walk down the road, and there will certainly be trips to the veterinarian.

First, get your puppy used to the lead. Fasten a light lead to his collar and let him drag it along. Do this only when you're supervising—you don't want the lead to snag on something. Then pick up the end of the lead.

Encourage your puppy to follow you by using a happy voice and treats. If your puppy stops or veers off in another direction, encourage him to return to you. Do not tug, pull, or yank at him. When your Dachshund understands that the lead is connecting the two of you, try short walks. If your Dachshund pulls, stop walking. He'll likely turn around and look at you, wondering

Short and Sweet

Keep your training sessions short and happy. Three or four short sessions of 5 minutes is more effective than one session of 20 minutes, especially with a puppy.

Once your Dachshund has learned what "sit" means, reinforce the training by asking him to do it many times during the day.

why you're not following. When the lead is slack, start walking again. If he pulls again, repeat the process. Don't yell, don't scream, and don't yank.

With or without a clicker, you can use treats to convince your Dachshund that walking next to you—or at least close enough to keep the lead slack—is a good idea. I keep my dog interested by randomly saying her name and throwing her a treat. Besides keeping her close, this is a good way to get her attention if there are distractions. If I see another person approaching walking a dog, I can say her name and offer a treat, and she is focusing on me instead of wanting to bark at the other dog.

Lead Styles

There are many different kinds of collars and leads on the

market. I prefer a soft, thin leather lead, but sometimes these are hard to find. Most pet supply shops will have cotton or nylon leads that work well. Six feet is a good length. Stay away from chain leads. You don't need one to control your Dachshund and, if you're holding it and your Dachshund suddenly dashes after a squirrel, the chain can tear the skin on your hand.

If you have a park to walk in, you may want to get a retractable lead to allow your Dachshund a bit more freedom. I find them annoying and awkward, but many people love them.

The thing to keep in mind is that most retractable leads allow your dog 15 to 25 feet (4.6 to 7.6m) of roaming room. Remember to bring your dog back to your side if other people or dogs are approaching. Not every person wants to say hello to your dog and not every approaching dog will be friendly. Your own dog may not be friendly. This is sometimes very hard for people to understand. Just because one dog loves everyone, including other dogs, doesn't mean the reverse is true. Keep your Dachshund under control and away from other dogs, especially if the other dog walker indicates that his dog is not friendly.

What is your lead attached to? Some leads come with a built-in collar: Just slip the loop over your dog's head and go. While these are great for getting your Dachshund from the house to the car, I don't like them for actual walks. For one thing, when they're loose, the loop can open to a size where a flip of the head sets your Dachshund free. If I'm using a one-piece collar and lead, I prefer the "show lead" type. These open up to easily slip over the dog's head, then a little sliding clip or bead tightens the collar so it fits snugly, but doesn't continue to tighten.

Choosing a Collar

A flat nylon or leather buckle collar will work well on your Dachshund. You really shouldn't need much more with a Dachshund, but you should know what else there is.

Let's start with the training collar. This may be made of chain or nylon, and consists of a ring that slides freely up and down the collar, and a ring that fastens to the lead. To correctly put this on your Dachshund, form the letter "P" with the collar. The straight part of the letter should be parallel to the ground, with the loop hanging free. If your Dachshund is on your left, slide the loop over his head. This allows the collar to hang loosely until you take up

"Leave It" or Lose It

Of course you're going to keep your belongings out of reach of curious puppies, and of course you'll just use dog toys and not old socks or shoes as toys for your dog. But, if your Dachshund should get a sock, a nylon stocking, or a slipper, the leave it command will prevent a crazy game of tag—and may also save your slipper.

the slack with the lead.

Another kind of collar is the martingale, which is made of two loops. One loop runs through the two rings of the first loop. This is easy to slip over your dog's head, and the top loop means you can draw the bottom loop closed so that it stays around your Dachshund's throat but can only be pulled closed so far. There's no danger of your Dachshund choking. If your Dachshund isn't wearing a collar all the time, this is a good type for taking walks because it is so easy to slip on and off.

Pinch collars have small prongs that point in, and when pulled tight, they pinch your dog's neck. These collars can be useful training tools for larger breeds, but there shouldn't be any reason to use one with a Dachshund.

Consider a Harness

It's possible that you won't want a collar at all, but instead will opt for a harness. A harness is a good choice if you're going to use some kind of seat belt system in your car instead of a crate. Many of these devices work better with a harness. However, when you're taking a walk, you'll have less control with a harness. It's all too easy for your dog to lean into the harness and pull, as there's nothing around his throat to slow him down. With a determined

Stand can be a useful request when you're bathing your Dachshund.

When you're playing with your Dachshund, you can teach him to "leave it" or "drop it" when you want him to release what he has in his mouth and let you have it.

Dachshund who has found a scent to follow and has decided not to listen to you, a harness may not be a good thing.

If you do decide on a harness, make sure that you buy the right size. Too loose or too tight, and it may rub and cause sores. Also, if you buy a harness before your Dachshund is full grown, make sure it's adjustable, or you'll need to buy another one as your dog grows. Either way, with collars and harnesses, keep an eye on the size. What fits your puppy will not work for your dog.

Another alternative is the head halter, which fits over your dog's head much like a horse's halter. This eliminates any choking or harm to your dog's throat, but some people feel that, used incorrectly, a head halter may cause disc damage to the neck and spine. Talk to your breeder, your other Dachshund-owning friends, and your veterinarian.

BASIC OBEDIENCE TRAINING

Training used to mean no treats, a training collar, a lead, and frequently pushing or pulling your dog into the position desired. Working this way, dogs learned to sit, stay down and many other things. But did they enjoy it? Did they ever understand about learning? Since we can't ask the dogs, we'll never know. As

Keep Training Fun for Both of You

No matter what method or combination of methods you use to train your Dachshund, remember to keep sessions short and positive. Three or four 5-minute sessions are better than one long session. Patience is also important. Don't lose your temper with your puppy, and have a sense of humour. Remember that even games can be a way to teach your dog. (Try putting your dog in a stay, going to another room, and calling him.) Don't expect too much at first, but eventually your Dachshund will be doing a sit-stay while you're out of sight.

training moves away from this method, it's important to remember that, used correctly, this method was not cruel. A dog was never corrected until he had learned a command, and, when he did obey, there was lavish praise, typically in a high, happy voice.

Today, most training methods focus more on food rewards. It seems to be more fun for both the dogs and the people, and certainly, with clicker training, dogs seem to understand the process of learning.

While it is not a good idea to start formal training, or even puppy classes, until your dog has had all his vaccinations, you can start some simple training at home. Most Dachshunds are chowhounds and can be motivated by food, especially soft treats. Just remember that the piece you offer doesn't have to be very large. You want a trained dog, not an overweight one.

Coming When Called

While you won't be doing formal recalls, your puppy should know his name and should come when called. Offer treats and call your puppy. Sound happy and excited. If his attention wanders, run away from your puppy, calling his name. When he comes, give him a treat and praise him. Never call your puppy for punishment or for something he may find unpleasant. Call him to dinner, not to show him an accident on the rug. If it's time to do his nails, go and get him and pick him up. No matter how frustrated the puppy may make you when you're in a hurry and he won't come in, when you do get him, be gentle and praise him. He must always associate good things with obeying the come command.

Teaching Sit

Sitting is probably the easiest thing you can teach a puppy. Hold a treat in front of the dog and slowly move it back over the top of his head. Don't hold it too high or he'll be tempted to jump up. As the treat moves back, give the sit command. The puppy will sit as he tries to follow the treat with his eyes and nose. The instant he sits, give him the treat and tell him how wonderful he is. Keep practicing until he will sit without the treat.

Teaching Stay

Next, you might want to teach your Dachshund to stay. Start with your Dachshund sitting on your left. Place your open palm in front of his nose and give the stay command. Move one step

The sit command is one of the easiest to teach your Dachshund, and serves as the foundation for several other commands and tricks.

directly in front of your Dachshund, then move back beside him and praise. Gradually extend the amount of time you are in front of him before you release him. As he seems to understand the command, move backward a step or two. If he breaks from the sit, gently replace him, repeat the stay command, and step away. Don't try to go too fast, don't lose your temper, and keep the lesson short and happy. Always end on a positive note.

Teaching Down

Down is a little harder. Many books and many instructors will tell you that once your dog is sitting, you just take a treat and slowly move it down toward his feet and out a bit. The dog will

It's All In the Timing

The most important aspect of clicker training is the timing. Whenever your puppy does something you want him to do, click and treat.

If you want to pursue more formal training with your Dachshund, you should search out a trainer you want to work with.

slide into the down. I've seen this work with many breeds, but I've also noticed that many small breeds just pop right up onto all four feet. I don't know if it's the short legs or what.

One of the best ways to teach down to a Dachshund is to teach him a few other commands first, so he understands the concept of learning something. If you have decided to use a clicker, this is one of the benefits. Dogs trained with a clicker seem to realise that there is something you want them to do. They will frequently try everything they know to get you to click and treat. Teach him a sit. Teach a stay. Teach him to walk nicely, even if you won't ever require a perfect heel position. Then, try a down.

First, tell your Dachshund to sit. Hold a treat in your hand, and move it slowly down and away as you give the command to down. If he slides into the down, terrific. Give him lots of praise and the treat. Instead of sliding into the down, he may jump up and go after the hand holding the treat. Don't let him get the treat. He may paw at your hand, or even nibble at it, trying to get the treat. He may sit again. Be patient. Eventually, he will lie down, and that's when you quickly give him the treat and praise him.

Teaching Stand

Stand also can be a useful command. You can use it when you're grooming your Dachshund, when he's at the veterinarian, or when he comes in with muddy feet and you want to wipe them off. If you think you might want to someday show your Dachshund in conformation, you'll need this skill. Standing for examination is also one of the obedience exercises.

When your Dachshund is seated, take a treat, show it to him, and move it forward from his nose a bit, saying, "Stand" at the same time. When he moves into the stand, praise him or click and give him the treat.

Train As You Play

Another way to teach your Dachshund is to name actions as you play with your Dachshund. If your Dachshund will fetch, throw a ball and tell him to "fetch" or "take it." When he brings it back, tell him to "leave it" or "drop it." Work on having him put it in your hand. You can do this with anything your dog may have—a toy, a bone, a sock. I teach my dogs to "leave it" with almost everything. If there's three feet of snow in the garden and a Dachshund has a toy in his mouth, you'll want him to leave that toy in the house before he goes out. You won't want to have to dig through the snow to find it, or let it stay hidden until it thaws. Also, if your dog happens to find a dead animal and decides he'd like to bring it indoors, you won't want to have to pry it from his jaws. You'll want him to leave it.

TRAINING WITH A CLICKER

Clicker training has become very popular and is a good way to train your puppy using only positive methods. Training clickers are available at most pet shops.

The clicker marks the behaviour at the instant it occurs. There's no delay, as there might be with a word of praise and a treat. Also, the clicker sound is the same every time. There's no edge of impatience, no variation in volume or tone. You can achieve the same results with a word instead of a click, but it has to be a word you only use when training, you have to say it immediately when the dog gives you the desired response,

Capturing Behaviour

"Capturing" occurs when you turn a dog's natural behaviour into a command. You see the dog do something, decide it's something you'd like him to do on command, and you click.

and you have to try to say it exactly the same way every time. A clicker is much easier.

In the Beginning

To start, get your puppy used to the idea that when he hears the click, he will get a treat. Click and treat several times so the puppy makes the connection between clicker and treat. This is called "charging the clicker," and it won't take long for your Dachshund to figure out the connection between a click and a treat.

You may want to start by luring your dog, that is, using food to lead, or lure, your dog into doing what you want—for instance, luring the dog into a sit by holding a treat slightly above and over his head. When he sits, click and give him the treat. It may take a little practice to get your timing right. Also, with clicker training, there is no coercion at all. No pressure on the neck or shoulders or rump, no positioning of the legs or body.

While this is a legitimate way to use the clicker, you don't want to always lure. If you only lure, your Dachshund won't offer behaviours on his own, which is what you want. You want your dog to be thinking about learning, which seems to be what happens with clicker training. You can almost see the light bulb go on over your dog's head when he realises that you want him to do something. He'll actively try to figure out just what that something is so that you'll click and treat.

Shaping Behaviour

Shaping a behaviour starts by watching your dog and clicking when he begins to do or does something you want him to do. For instance, you want to teach your Dachshund to lie down on a specific rug or mat. If it helps, you can put your Dachshund on a lead to keep him in the area, but no hauling or guiding. Just stand there with your dog on a loose lead. If your Dachshund walks over the mat, click and treat. If he happens to sit or lie down, click and give more treats.

The first time or two, you may be rewarding just the walking over the mat, but eventually he will realise that being on the mat earns him treats. Then treat only when he sits, and finally, only when he lies down. If you've taught him to sit and down earlier, chances are he'll be trying these behaviours to see if he gets a reward. Name the action by saying, "Go to your place" or "Go to bed" or whatever you want to say. Remember to be consistent.

The thing to remember about clicker training is that you must click when your dog is doing the behaviour you want. If you have an instructor in your area who uses clicker training, talk to her about how to use it best. Read a book or two on the subject. It may take you a while to learn it yourself, but it will work, and it won't take your Dachshund long to understand it. Besides basic

Training your dog to sit when greeting other people, or even other dogs, is extremely beneficial.

obedience, clicker training can be used in agility training as well as almost any other area of dog training.

Remember that you'll need lots of treats if you're clicker training. I cut up lots of a soft treat into tiny little bits. Cheese, hot dogs, or baked chicken are all good choices. It's not unusual to go through 30 to 50 tiny treats in a session. Vary the number of treats you give, as well. Don't always give just one. If your dog has mastered a new behaviour, give him a "jackpot." That is, give him five or six treats, one at a time. Next time, go back to one, then maybe two. This keeps your dog alert and eager.

Don't get frustrated if you can't seem to coordinate your clicking and your treating at first. With practice, you'll improve. It's not unusual to treat and click at first, and it's not a major crime. Your dog will continue to learn, even if you're not perfect. Pretty soon, you will have conditioned yourself to click or praise and treat. The last time I went to a groomer to get my dog's nails cut, I said thank you and dropped a dog treat into her hand!

TRAINING BEYOND THE BASICS

With patience, your dog's favourite treat, and a good book or two, you should be able to teach household manners to your dog. If more formal training appeals to you, you can start it on your own, but eventually, if you are thinking of any of the performance sports, you will want to find a professional trainer to help you. Class situations are a good way to both socialise your dog and get him used to distractions. If you've gotten to the point where you want a formal class setting, or want a trainer to come to you for private lessons, do some homework of your own before you sign up for lessons.

Finding a Class

First, decide what kind of a class you want. Do you just want to teach your dog to sit, stay, come, and walk on a slack lead? Are you hoping to use your dog for therapy work? Are you after more structured lessons that will prepare you for competition-level

The Language of Learning

Sometimes dogs seem to pick up more with body language than with verbal cues. If you lean forward when you are teaching the sit, your dog may sit whenever you stand in front of him and lean forward, without the spoken word "sit."

Anxiety Barking

If the problem is that your dog barks when no one is home, it may be because he is anxious. This can take a long time to correct. Start by leaving the house. Close the door, then re-enter immediately. Praise the dog and treat. Leave again. Count to five. Go back in. This is a slow process, but eventually, your dog will realise that you are not leaving for good.

Be careful not to let the pack—or a pack mentality—take over.

obedience? Does agility appeal to you? In obedience, your dog works close to you most of the time. In agility, your dog works away from you. Think about what you want from a class before you waste time and money on lessons that don't meet your needs.

Many local clubs sponsor training lessons. In my hometown, the animal shelter offers regular 8-week sessions. Pet superstores or boarding kennels may offer classes as well. Before you enrol, get some information on the instructor. How long have they been teaching? What breed of dog do they have? What methods do they use in training? Clicker training is gaining in popularity, and if you find a good instructor it's a wonderful way to train your dog, but there are other methods that work as well.

If possible, see if you can attend a class as an observer. What is the instructor like with the dogs? Stay away from anyone who advocates hitting the dog or lifting him off his feet by the lead. Your Dachshund doesn't need that, and neither do you.

How large is the class? The larger the class, the less individual attention you'll receive. Classes of more than 10 or 12 dogs might work if the dogs are already trained to some degree and are working on advanced training, but for beginners, the smaller the class, the better. This is true for agility training as

Watching how dogs interact and play with each other can teach you how to communicate better with them.

well. The larger the class, the less time you and your Dachshund will have to practice.

Talk to friends and neighbours who have taken obedience classes. See if your veterinarian knows of a class. If you want private lessons, get referrals. Talk to people who've hired a particular instructor.

Once you've signed up for a class, try to attend every session, and do your homework. One training session a week will not teach your Dachshund what you want him to know. You have to devote the time to daily training sessions. But remember, in spite of your care in selecting your trainer, if things aren't working—if the trainer is too rough, or doesn't control the class and you feel your dog might be in danger, or for any reason you are uncomfortable or unhappy—leave. You may not get a refund, but your dog's well-being should be your first concern.

PROBLEM BEHAVIOURS

Digging

There may be times when your Dachshund does something you'd rather he didn't do. Many times a sharp "no!" or redirecting the dog to something that is permitted will take care of the problem. Almost all puppies will dig a bit, but it's something they usually outgrow.

Dachshunds, of course, are supposed to dig, and they may dig their entire lives. If your dog enjoys digging, designate a special area of the garden for digging. You might even want to create his own little sandbox. If he digs outside of his special spot, distract him with a toy and lead him to the correct spot. Lightly bury a few smelly treats in the permitted spot and when he digs them up, praise him. Sometimes dogs dig because they are bored. Play with your dog in the garden, or supply a toy or a bone that he enjoys.

Jumping Up

Jumping can be a bad habit, and one that is easily learned. People with small dogs usually don't mind if their dog jumps on them. Dachshunds are small and generally won't knock you down. It's easier to pet a small dog when he jumps up. But you might not be as happy about the jumping if you're wearing good clothes and your Dachshund has muddy feet. Besides, let's face it, not all your friends will think your dog is as cute as you do. Teach your dog to jump up on you on command, if you want to. Otherwise, discourage him. If you have a friend or relative who is a frequent visitor, get them to help.

If your Dachshund jumps up, have your friend turn sideways and ignore the dog. Tell your dog to sit. When he does, have your friend pet him. Only give him attention when he sits, not when he is jumping. Dachshunds love attention. If you pay attention to him when he jumps up, you are reinforcing that behaviour.

Barking

Dachshunds have a good, sharp warning bark, and any dog may bark out of boredom if he is left alone too long. Your Dachshund shouldn't be left outdoors unattended for long periods of time, but if he barks every time he is in the garden, even if for only a few minutes, it can become annoying. Consider installing a solid fence. Dogs rarely bark at things they can't see. If that's not possible, consider planting shrubs to screen the pavement or neighbour's garden. Give your dog interesting toys, or play with him yourself when he's in the garden.

Many people use invisible fencing and like it very much, but for a small dog, I prefer tangible fencing of some kind. Invisible fencing may very well keep your Dachshund in your garden, but it won't keep out a stray that might wander by. Dachshunds are just like any other dog; they will probably bark at passing dogs, and

Ignoring Bad Behaviour

One method of discouraging unwanted behaviour is to completely ignore it. If your dog jumps up to greet you, turn away from him, fold your arms across your chest, and do not make eye contact. Only respond to the behaviour you want, such as sitting or moving away. Respond calmly, so as not to excite your dog into other unwanted behaviours.

Dachshunds communicate with each other and with us using all their senses.

they will defend their territory. Unfortunately, their size means they will more than likely lose a battle with a larger dog. Fence your garden with fencing tall enough to keep out bigger dogs who might be a threat to your dog.

Indoors, if your Dachshund is barking more than you'd like, there are a couple of ways you can curb the barking. One way is to teach your dog to bark on command. Once he knows how to bark on command, you also can teach a command to stop the barking. When your dog barks, click and treat. Name the action. Then choose a word that tells him to be quiet. When he does stop, click and treat. If your dog barks every time someone comes to the door, get a friend to help you by coming to the door. You may appreciate the fact that your dog lets you know someone is at the door, but then he should stop when you tell him to. Have your friend knock on the door. When your Dachshund stops barking at your command, open the door. Have your friend treat your dog. Repeat the process.

Challenging Pack Position

As was mentioned, dogs are pack animals. Sometimes dogs try to take over as pack leader. They may refuse to move when you want them to. They may growl or snarl if they are in a chair or on a bed and you want to move them. They may become very possessive of food or toys. You'll need to take back the leadership. This means your dog gets nothing for free; he must earn everything. He must sit and stay before he eats. He must wait until you go through a door—and no more sleeping on the bed.

If your dog is genuinely aggressive, possessive over food or what he sees as his territory, or if he snaps or growls at family members, see your veterinarian first. Your pet may not appear to be in pain, but if there's a physical problem, he may be snapping or growling to warn you away from touching a particular area of his body that hurts. If there's nothing wrong with your Dachshund physically, you may want to contact an animal behaviour specialist, which is not the same as a dog trainer. There are many good trainers who are not behaviour specialists. Depending on the

If your dog is licking his nose, yawning, or shaking himself, he is using signals to break the tension. Look around to see what might have him worried.

severity of the problem, a good trainer may be able to help you, even if she isn't a behaviour specialist.

If you find you really need a behaviour specialist, start your search by talking to your veterinarian and people at your local club. Unfortunately, there is no national standard for certification at this point, so you'll need to consider credentials and get references. Ask to talk to former clients of the specialist. Other helpful organisations include The Association of Pet Behaviour Counsellors.

LEARNING EVERYDAY WORDS

Dogs can learn the meaning of many of the words we use everyday. They easily learn the commands we teach, like "sit," "stay," "down," "come," "wait," "off," "take it," and "leave it." If we make the effort, they'll learn to respond to words like "shake," "roll over," "high five," "beg," and any number of other words. People who run their Dachshunds in agility have taught their dogs the names of the obstacles, such as "tunnel" and "chute."

Without our making any effort at all, our dogs quickly learn words like "dinner," and "biscuit," and "walk." They know the words "bed time," and many, many more. My parents had a very sensitive dog who, as a puppy, enjoyed digging holes in

the garden. My parents scolded him, telling him, "no digging." He was so affected by the words that for the rest of his life, my parents had to spell the words "dig" and "digging" or he would think he was being scolded.

Service dogs learn many commands specific to the needs of their owners. We all can agree that our dogs know at least some verbal language. And we know some of theirs. If our dog whines, we may know he wants to go out, or that he is afraid of thunder. If he barks and stares at the cupboard door, he wants a dog biscuit. When your dog drops a toy at your feet and looks expectantly at you, you know he wants you to throw the toy. But what about other types of communication? What about body language? Dogs are masters at interpreting body language. They "read" other dogs as well as humans. Let's start with a dog's body language; what they can tell from looking at another dog, and what you can learn by watching theirs.

Not all dogs have tails, and some tails just don't function quite like others. There are certain tail positions that can tell you about what a dog is feeling or thinking. A dog with his tail tucked between his legs may be frightened. He is definitely being submissive. He also may be unhappy or unsure of himself. He is telling other dogs—and you, if you are paying attention—that he is no threat to anyone. He also will avert his eyes, plaster his ears back, and hold his head low.

A dog also may be anxious or stressed in this position, and he may be panting.

Dogs who are worried also may sit with one paw raised. A yawn briefly lowers a dog's blood pressure and helps him stay calm. A friend's dog licks his nose repeatedly if he meets another dog on a walk. If she continues to approach the strange dog, or the strange dog gets too close, her dog will snarl and snap. She now recognises his nose-licking signal, and prevents meeting other dogs.

If a dog is aggressive, everything about him leans forward and gets bigger. Ears will be up and forward, and the dog will be on his toes. His hackles will rise. His tail will be upright and stiff. If the dog is snarling, his nose will be wrinkled. He will be staring. If you meet a dog like this on a walk, don't let your Dachshund say hello. This dog does not want to play. If your dog exhibits these traits, don't let him approach another dog.

Your dog may nudge your hand or lean against you in an effort to get you to pet him, or he may put his paw on your knee. A quick lick on your face means he loves you and recognises you as the leader. Some dogs will limp as a way to get your attention, especially if they've ever suffered a leg or paw injury and had you fuss over them.

Body Language

Dogs use a play bow to indicate that they are in the mood for a game. They'll use this with both people and other dogs. In a play bow, the front half of the body is lowered so that the forelegs are on the ground, leaving the rear end in the air. The tail will be wagging and the dog may give a high-pitched bark or two. He may pant. If your dog drops a toy at your feet and gives you a play bow, it's time to take a break and enjoy your dog.

The play bow can work both ways. You can play bow to your dog when you want to have a game. Put your hands on your knees, smile, pant, and widen your eyes. I've gotten my dog to respond when she's on the bed by putting my arms flat on the bed and lowering my head. Just remember that if your dog responds to that, it will be with a quick pounce, so be ready to dodge.

Some forms of communication are only between dogs. When male dogs mark bushes and trees and poles with urine they are leaving a message to other dogs about their size, sex, and attitude. Females mark to a lesser extent, but they are also leaving a message. Sniffing their way along a walk is the doggy equivalent of reading a newspaper.

Dogs also love to roll in anything that smells different. If you're lucky, your dog will roll in a patch of mint. If you're not so lucky it will be a dead fish—or worse. Some say that rolling in something pungent is a form of camouflage; dogs are using the scent of another creature to disguise themselves. That may be true, but sometimes I think they just like smells. My male routinely rolls on my husband's shoes.

As much as dogs depend on body language to communicate with other dogs, they are also close observers of human body language. Standing tall and looming over a dog is a sign of dominance when another dog does it, and also when you do it. When you stand tall, or lean over your dog, or even put your arm across his back, you are saying you are dominant; that you are the boss. Conversely, if a strange dog is nervous and shy, you can help the introductions along by crouching down, turning sideways to appear smaller, and not making eye contact. Staring is a form of both dominance and aggression.

Obedience competitors have to be very careful not to move in a certain way, as it may be a cue to the dog. Even the slight drop of a shoulder can be a cue to a dog. That's why hand signals are often incorporated into training. The dog quickly learns both cues. I've noticed that my own dog, when heeling, will sometimes wait to sit until I turn my head slightly. It was an unconscious gesture on my part, but she quickly learned that it means sit.

Chapter

ADVANCED TRAINING AND ACTIVITIES

for Your Dachshund

Y ou may never want to do more with your Dachshund than have him accompany you on your walks around the neighbourhood or travels around the world. But it's nice to know that there are many other activities in which you and your Dachshund can participate and even compete.

The Dachshund was bred to be a tenacious hunting dog, going after such fierce vermin as badgers in their lairs. These instincts live on in your dog, and he has a strong prey drive along with a "bring it on" attitude when it comes to a challenge. This may make some advanced training you take on more difficult than if you were working with a retriever or spaniel (dogs bred to be more in service to their owners), but it makes the accomplishments particularly rewarding.

The activities in which you and your Dachshund can compete range from a basic good manners test to highly competitive field trials. This chapter will introduce you to those activities. If they interest you, check the resources in the back of this book for the contact information and get involved. You and your Dachshund will really enjoy it.

CANINE GOOD CITIZEN SCHEME

This is a scheme run by the Kennel Club that is designed to reward dogs who have good manners at home and in the community. The programme stresses responsible pet ownership for owners and basic good manners for dogs.

The scheme was launched in 1992. Since then, over 52,000 dogs have passed the test, which is administered through more than 1,000 training organisations.

*One of the things a
Dachshund who's
competing in obedience
must have mastered is the
sit-stay command.*

Any dog is eligible to take part in the Good Citizen Dog Scheme, which is a noncompetitive plan that trains owners and dogs for everyday situations. There are four awards - bronze, silver, gold and puppy foundation assessment - which are based on the level of training that both dog and owner have reached together.

For more information contact the Kennel Club at www.the-kennel-club.org.uk. This is a great opportunity to develop the bond between dog and owner. You'll both benefit!

Earning a Dood Citizen award isn't hard, but it does take preparation and training. Training for the awards is training for good manners and responsible behaviour as well as basic skills every performance dog should know.

Good Citizen awards are designed to measure just how well-behaved and well-mannered your dog is. You will need a regular buckle collar and lead for the test, but you may not use head halters, harnesses, pinch collars or any other kind of collars or leads. Most of the exercises are performed with your Dachshund on the lead. You will also need your dog's regular brush or comb. You may not use any treats or toys as incentive during the test.

If your dog doesn't pass a test, he can take it again on another occasion. A dog will not pass a test if he doesn't complete any of the exercises, or if he growls, snaps, lunges or bites at the tester or anyone else who is helping in the test.

The exercises become progressively more difficult as you work through bronze, silver and gold levels. The

Treats are an excellent motivator when training your Dachshund, but be careful not to overfeed him.

preliminary exercises are very straightforward and include the following:

1. Accepting a friendly stranger
2. Sitting politely for petting
3. Appearance and grooming
4. Out for a walk (walking on a loose lead)
5. Walking through a crowd
6. Sit and down on command and staying in place
7. Coming when called
8. Reaction to another dog
9. Reaction to distraction
10. Supervised separation

And that's it! Do you think your Dachshund could pass these steps? If not (yet), start training for this test as a goal. Practise each step until your Dachshund is comfortable doing them all. It feels great to earn a Good Citizen award, and you can take pride in knowing that you have a canine good citizen as part of your family.

Working With Distractions

The group exercises are one of the reasons a class situation is helpful. Besides getting your dog used to other dogs, your instructor may introduce distractions to proof your dog. The instructor may bounce a ball, knock over a chair, or walk another dog across the floor. If your dog can handle classroom distractions without breaking his sit or stay, the odds are he will remain in position in the ring.

COMPETITIVE OBEDIENCE

If your dog passes the Canine Good Citizen Scheme or if you have been enjoying obedience classes, you may want to consider earning obedience titles. Most Dachshunds are so food motivated that basic obedience training is fairly quick, but they also get bored easily. Keep training sessions short and positive. If you have not been taking formal classes, you may want to consider them if you are going to compete in competitive obedience. An instructor will know the best way to teach specific exercises, and attending classes will get your dog used to other dogs. Also, when practicing the long sits and downs, it is better to do so in a group as it simulates actual trial conditions.

The real joy, the true joy, of competing in obedience is the bonding that occurs between you and your dog while preparing for competition. You work as a team, and you know what to expect from each other. The sheer amount of one-on-one time involved in training builds a bond that becomes stronger during every session.

There are various levels of obedience in the UK, with each covering a range of abilities. These are pre-beginners, beginners, novice, class A, class B and class C. Each level becomes progressively more demanding. There will be a winner in each level of class.

The pre-beginners class is for the least experienced in the obedience world. Competitors must perform five different obedience exercises, including walking to heel, both on and off lead, recall, sit-stay, and down-stay.

The beginners class is for those who have succeeded at pre-beginners. This class includes all the exercises from the pre-beginners class but also includes retrieving an article.

The novice class contains all the elements from the beginners class, and also includes temperament test, in which the judge will run his hands over the dog.

Class A is similar to the novice class, although the exercises are longer and less encouragement is

Taking Home a Title

In the US in 2004, 51 Dachshunds earned Companion Dog titles; 10 earned Companion Dog Excellent titles; and 1 earned a Utility Dog title. Will your dog be next?

With time and dedication, your Dachshund can become a champion.

allowed from the handler. There is also a scent discrimination test.

Class B is more involved than Class A. There is an additional exercise in which the handler must send the dog away, order him to drop to the floor, then call him back. There are also exercises for the retrieve, scent discrimination, sit-stay, down-stay and stand-stay.

Class C is the master class of obedience competition. Many of the exercises are longer in duration and the judges allow less room for error. The handler must also get the dog to perform six different exercises while dog and handler are at least ten paces apart.

There are three types of obedience tests or shows - limited shows, open shows, and championship shows. Competition becomes successively more difficult through these tests. There may be many different classes scheduled at each show, from pre-beginners through to Class C.

Championship classes are open to anyone and they offer a special award - the Kennel Club's obedience challenge certificate. These certificates are available only to dogs winning in class C events. Once a dog has achieved three obedience challenge certificates or 'tickets' under three different judges, he is awarded the title Obedience Champion.

RALLY OBEDIENCE

Rallly Obedience is a new event that is taking America by storm. It is run by the American Kennel Club. Although it is not yet recognised in the UK, it's propularity in the US means it is likely to make an apearance here before long.

Rally Obedience is a combination of agility and obedience, though emphasis is less on speed and precision and more on how well dogs and handlers perform together as a team. It was created with the average dog owner in mind, to help promote a positive human / canine relationship with an emphasis on fun and excitement. It also takes the pressure off of competing, while still allowing owners to showcase their Dachshunds' obedience skills.

In Rally Obedience, the dog and handler move through a course that has been designed by the rally judge. They proceed at their own pace through a course of designated stations - between 10 and 20, depending on the level. A sign at each of these stations provides instructions on the skill that is to be performed, such as "Halt and Sit", "Halt", "Sit", "Down", "Right Turn", "About Turn" or "Perform a 270-degree left turn while heeling".

Getting Gloves

Sets of three Dachshund-sized gloves may be purchased from catalogues or booths at dog shows, so you don't need to worry about your Dachshund tripping on a huge work glove or about buying two pairs of gloves and throwing one glove away.

THE CONFORMATION RING (DOG SHOWS)

Conformation judging is what most people think of when they think of a dog show. The Group and Best in Show judging is what you see on television when a show such as Crufts is televised. Dog shows are held year round, indoors and out, and may range in size from entries of under 100 to over 3,000.

Over 7,000 canine events are licensed by the Kennel Club each year and these are managed by around 2,000 dog clubs in the UK.

If you are very serious about showing your dog it is advisable to join a breed club and they will be a great source of information and expert advice on your breed. More information can be found at the Kennel Club website, www.the-kennel-club.org.uk.

Is Your Dog Show Quality?

At a dog show, your Dachshund will be evaluated against the judge's idea of an ideal Dachshund according to the breed's standard.

You might not have thought much about showing your Dachshund when you got him, but chances are your breeder discussed with you whether or not your puppy was potentially show quality. Show quality means your dog has no disqualifying faults as discussed in the standard, and that he is structurally sound and built as a Dachshund should be. Another quality to look for in a show dog is personality. Most Dachshunds have plenty of

personality, but some may be a bit more laid back than others. A competitive show dog loves the crowd and has attitude. You will sometimes hear a judge say that a particular dog was "asking for the win." That is a dog who is confident and happy in the ring. If you think you might enjoy showing, ask your breeder or someone who knows Dachshunds to reevaluate him. If their opinion is positive, give it a try!

Many clubs offer handling classes, and this is an excellent place to learn about how to gait and stack your dog and what kind of collar and lead to use, as well as bait (the food used to get a dog's attention in the ring). With my first show dog I had both a mentor in the breed of the dog, and I also attended classes in handling. The formal class gave my dog socialisation with other dogs and I received pointers on how to place my dog on the table, move at the proper pace, and learn the different patterns of movement that the judge might request. (In order to see your dog in action, the judge may ask for a down and back, a triangle, or an L. You'll want to practice this before you actually show your dog.)

Whether or not you attend formal classes, you may want to attend a match or two before you actually enter a show. A match is an event put on by a dog club. It is run like a dog show, but the dogs can't win any points. It is frequently more casual than a show, and a judge at a match is more likely to give you advice than a judge at a licensed show would. Match entry fees are also much less than those of a show.

Preparing for the Show Ring

When I first started showing, my mentor gave me breed-specific tips in terms of what kind of collar and lead work best, a good speed to move at for gaiting, and ideas for bait. My mentor showed me how to groom for the ring, helped me with entry forms, and suggested judges who might like my dog. This last tip can definitely help you save time and money. An experienced dog show competitor keeps a file on judges and what they may or may not like in a particular dog. If your dog's movement is not the best, there's no point in showing to a judge who considers movement very important. If your dog's head fits the standard in every way, there is probably a judge who is looking for just that feature.

Another advantage to having a mentor is that you and she can travel together to your first few shows. It's a lot less intimidating

Conformation Eligibility

To compete in conformation dogs must:

• Be registered with the Kennel Club (or other relevant organisation);
• Not have any disqualifying faults according to the Dachshund standard;
• Be a minimum age of six months;
• Be in mandated show trim;
• Cannot be spayed or neutered.

Find a Mentor

As with other dog-related activities, it is possible to learn from books and from trial and error, but it is much, much easier if you can find someone to help you. A dog show mentor can save you time and money and may mean the difference between giving up and persevering.

when you are travelling with someone who knows where to go and what to do.

At a Show

So, let's pretend to do just that...go to a show. You've purchased the proper show lead, as recommended by your mentor, and you've attended classes, so you understand how to move your dog at the correct pace around the ring and how to stack your dog on the table, so the judge can examine him. You've cooked hot dogs or liver or chicken, or whatever treats your dog loves, so that you can get his attention in the ring. Your dog is also in good show condition—well groomed and physically ready. A Dachshund isn't a working dog, but he still should not be soft and flabby. He should get enough regular daily exercise to give him good muscle tone.

Packing for the Show

It's time to pack the car for the show. The most important item, of course, is your dog. But how is he to travel? You'll need his crate in the car, and you may want an extra one for your hotel room and maybe even one at the show site. Pack your tack box, which holds all your grooming supplies: Brushes, treats, show leads, spray bottles of water, baby wipes, waterless shampoo, and whatever else you need to make sure your dog looks his best for the judge. You'll need your grooming table, a grooming smock, and don't forget extra towels. You'll want one for on the grooming table, one for wiping off mud, drying feet, (or maybe drying the entire dog if it rains), and a couple for extra bedding in case what is in the crate gets dirty; you can never have too many towels.

A wire exercise pen is a good idea, too, so your Dachshund has a place other than his crate to move around in, and if the grounds are muddy or very crowded, he has a place for relieving himself without the need for a walk.

Table Breeds

The Dachshund is a table breed, meaning that at a dog show the judge examines him on a grooming table. The judge also watches the dog move and stand on the ground.

Water is also essential. Carry your own water from home to prevent any digestive upset. If the show is in the summer, make sure you have whatever you need to keep your Dachshund cool. There are wonderful crate pads that keep pets cool, as well as special little coats you can wet down to keep your Dachshund from overheating. Some people use ice packs wrapped in a towel.

You'll also want to take food, of course, if you are going for more than one day. You may want to carry some for yourself as

Handling classes, mentors, and fellow dog show friends can all help you learn to handle and evaluate your Dachshund for the show ring.

well as the dog. Dog show food is usually of the hot dog and hamburger variety, if it exists at all. A small cooler packed with some sandwiches or snacks can make your day more pleasant.

What Will You Wear?

Consider your wardrobe as you pack. You want to look neat and well groomed, but you also should be prepared for whatever weather you may encounter. At an indoor show, this isn't as much of a concern, but at an outdoor show, you may encounter heat, cold, rain, mud, and/or wind. Follow the Scout motto and be prepared.

Don't forget your paperwork. You'll also want your judging schedule, so you'll know where you're supposed to be and at what time, and your dog's entry form, which is usually your ticket to enter the show. Remember to take any directions you need to get to the show site, and allow yourself plenty of time to get there. You've paid to enter your dog in the show; make sure you don't miss your ring time.

When You Get to the Show

You've made your list, checked it twice, and the car is loaded and ready to go. If you are going to an indoor show, there usually will be an unloading area near a building door. You can unload your grooming table and supplies, and then move your car to the parking area. It is a good idea to get to the show site early because grooming space fills up fast. Luckily, Dachshunds don't take up much room! At an outdoor show, the grooming area usually will be under a separate tent. Again, there will be a loading and unloading area. If the show site offers large, grassy parking areas with shade, you might want to simply set up your table next to your car so you can work out of the car and avoid unloading everything.

If you decide on this method, make sure you have some sort of awning or sunscreen to keep the car cool. Draping space blankets over the windows keeps out a lot of heat. Never, ever leave your dog unattended in a closed car. Dogs do not perspire like humans do. Their lungs act as a cooling agent. If they are breathing in super hot air, there is no chance for the proper heat exchange, and they will quickly overheat.

Don't even think about entering your dog in a show if he is not groomed to perfection, as this miniature Wirehaired is.

Once you're settled, indoors or out, double-check your judging time and find your ring, so you know exactly where you'll be going.

The next thing to do is groom your dog. You already should

What to Wear When Showing

You must look neat and well groomed when you show, but you also should be prepared for the weather. Throw your raincoat in the car, no matter what the long-range weather forecast says. Carry extra shoes and a hat. Flat, comfortable shoes are a must for both men and women; you don't want to risk falling in the ring, and you're going to be on your feet for most of the day, so you don't want tired feet.

Men should wear a blazer and tie; women should wear a dress or skirt, although a trousers suit is acceptable. Skirts should be loose enough to move freely in, without being too full. A billowing skirt can obscure the judges' view of your dog, and may even interrupt your dog's gait if the skirt blows across his face. Solid colours that make a good contrasting background to your dog are a good choice. With Dachshunds, greens, light-to-medium blues, and reds are good choices, and with red or cream Dachshunds, the darker colours make a good background. If you have a black Dachshund, avoid black or navy blue.

If you're showing in a performance event, you'll still want those comfortable shoes, but women generally wear trousers for performance events. In obedience, contrary to the conformation ring, wear trousers that match the colour of your Dachshund as closely as possible. A crooked sit may not be as noticeable if that black Dachshund is next to black trousers.

Agility competition is a little more casual in terms of dress. Wear something you can easily move in as you sprint from obstacle to obstacle. I've seen people compete barefoot and wearing shorts. Whatever works for you and your dog is fine.

have clipped your dog's toenails and foot fur at home, and given him a bath if needed. Show-site grooming for a Dachshund should be a matter of touch-up. Brush and comb thoroughly. If the site is muddy or wet, use waterless shampoo to spot clean. Wipe your dog's feet. Check his eyes, nose, and ears.

Next, you may want to crate your dog until just before you go to the ring, or you may want to head for your ring early. Some dogs show better if they go directly from their crate to the ring; others do better if they have a little time to settle down and get used to the crowd before showing. Experience will tell you which your dog will prefer. Either way, with or without your dog, try to watch the judge as he judges a few dogs so that you'll be ready for whatever pattern will be used when you gait your dog for him. Does he ask for the first dog to be put directly on the table, or will he ask you to go around the ring first? Knowing ahead of time will save time in the ring and make you calmer, which will help both you and your dog.

How Dog Shows Work

Dog shows can seem pretty complicated when you first attend one and try to work out what is going on, even as a spectator. But this is a highly organised sport. Dogs are trying to earn that coveted title of champion, and to do this, a dog must earn three

Going to several shows as an observer will help you feel more prepared when it's your turn as an exhibitor.

Challenge Certificates under three different judges. Challenge Certificates are on offer only at Championship shows, and in these competitions the best male and female will be awarded a CC.

In a dog show, dogs are individually exhibited by their handlers. This can be the pet owner, the breeder, or a professional handler. In the US, professional handlers are used in high-profile dog shows, but in the UK most Dachshunds are handled by their owners. Handlers bring the dogs out into the ring and the judge examines each one, and also watches all the dogs move around the ring together. Typically, the judge eliminates all but a handful at first, then even more carefully studies the finalists.

At the first level, dogs are divided into classes, and in each class, males and females are judged separately. Rosettes will be awarded to dogs in the highest places. When the judge has finished judging all the classes, it is time to find the overall winners.

The judge must look at his class winners and select the best male and the best female. This is no easy task, as he will be evaluating dogs from different ages, from puppies of a mere six months of age, right up to advanced, experienced show dogs. A number of dogs may already be Champions, so it is a very tough challenge for young, upcoming dogs to come forward.

The judge will make his choice and will select his winning male and female. If Challenge Certificates are on offer, both dogs will be awarded a CC. However, there is one final honour the breed judge can award - and that is Best of Breed. The judge will

The Dachshund's enthusiasm and "can-do" attitude make him an able peformer in agility.

138

Showing in the US

To earn an American Kennel Club Champion title, a dog must beat other dogs in multiple age and gender classes to become Winners Dog or Winners Bitch. Based on how many dogs are beaten, points, up to a maximum of five at one time, are earned. Some of the points won must be "majors", in which the dog earns three or more points in a single-breed class. A total of fifteen points, with two majors, are necessary to become a Champion of Record.

make a thorough evaluation of each dog, and will then declare a Best of Breed.

In a breed show, the Best of Breed winner is equivalent to winning Best in Show. But in an all-breed show, the Best of Breed (BOB) still has a way to go. The next step is to compete in the Group ring. For Dachshunds, that means your winning BOB Dachshund goes into the ring with all the other Hound breeds.

That means the best Dachshund will compete against the best Beagle, Basset and all the other best of breeds in the Hound Group. People wonder how a judge can choose between different breeds, but the dogs aren't really being judged against each other. They are each being evaluated according to how well each dog meets his own breed standard. This is a tough job for a judge because they have to be well acquainted with all the standards and be able to decide which dog best meets his own standard.

The best hound will then be awarded Best of Group. Meanwhile, in other rings, each Best of Breed in every other category is competing for their own Best of Group in each of the seven breed groups: Sporting, Gundog, Working, Terrier, Toy, Utility, and Pastoral.

But the fun isn't over yet! The ultimate honour in a dog show is to win Best in Show, and in a large all-breed dog show, this is quite an accomplishment. The seven Best in Group finalists enter the ring, and a Best in Show judge has the difficult task of choosing which among them - from a Chihuahua to Newfoundland - best meets its individual breed standard. One dog is awarded Best in Show (BIS). Breeders consider the number of BIS titles won in a dog's career a serious indicator of quality for breeding stock, and indeed it is. Because remember, that is the original point of this whole complicated event. A Dachshund puppy with multiple

Agility is the fastest-growing canine sport because both people and dogs love it.

BIS parents is probably going to be as excellent an example of a Dachshund, as it is meant to be.

Even if your dog doesn't win, you'll want to watch the entire Dachshund judging, and to cheer on the Best of Breed winner when he competes in the group ring.

AGILITY

If you can barely get your dog to heel, or obedience just doesn't sound like your cup of tea, don't worry; there are lots of other things you can do with your Dachshund!

For example, you might want to try agility, a rapidly growing sport that gives both you and your dog exercise in a fun way. Again, it's a good idea to find a class and a good instructor. Agility equipment takes up a lot of room and is fairly expensive to purchase, although if you are at all handy you can build most of it yourself.

About the Obstacles

The main obstacles in an agility course are the A-frame, where the dog goes up one side of the A and down the other; the dog walk, which is a sloping board that leads up to another level board across which the dog walks, and then another sloping board down to the ground; a seesaw; four types of jumps (water, rising spread, tyre and long jump); a pause table, where you must, at the judge's direction, either have your dog sit or down for a count of five; a pipe tunnel; and a collapsible tunnel, or chute, which consists of an open, rigid entry area, and an expanse of cloth for the exit. The fabric has no support, so the dog must push through it to exit.

Weave poles are the final element. The A-frame, the dog walk, and the seesaw are all contact obstacles; that is, they all have a contact zone where the obstacle touches the ground, usually painted yellow. The dog must touch this area as he gets both on and off of the obstacle. This is to ensure that the dog does not leap on or off the obstacle, thus risking injury.

What Makes an Agility Dog?

What does it take to make an agility dog? A natural aptitude is just the start. Next comes a lot of training and practise. Training, even for a fun sport like agility, must be enjoyable if a Dachshund is going to succeed. The Dachshund thrives on variety, so try not to practise the same sequence repetitively.

Possible problem areas for the Dachshund include a down-stay on the low pause table, which may be perceived as threatening for the small dog. A-frames are mountainous and may likewise take some extra work. But most Dachshunds, particularly the more slimly built dogs, are good jumpers and need very little instruction to get going. They love to jump and tackle the obstacles and take part in all the excitement of the agility course.

Dachshunds and their people can have tremendous fun competing to earn some of the agility titles that are on offer. Remember, it is not all about the winning, but on having a sense of accomplishment and fun.

When You're Hooked

Agility is a very challenging and complex sport, but as your dog gains confidence, he will perform with almost the same speed that he chases a ball. This speed can be a problem at advanced levels

The Agile Dachshund

Dachshunds are one of the breeds in the Hound Group that most actively competes in Agility.

because the dog may miss the yellow contact zone coming off an obstacle. The best advice is to put in the time in the early stages, making sure you get a solid contact, so that this does not become a problem at advanced levels. It's also a good idea to wait a bit and not push the dog too hard. A dog may not compete in agility until he is 18 months old. This gives both you and your dog time to get in condition and build up stamina. If you plan to do agility, the weave poles are an obstacle you will definitely want to have in your own garden. For competitive agility, one class a week is not enough to teach your dog proficiency on the weave poles. A few jumps are also a good idea.

TRACKING

Tracking is another activity you might want to try with your Dachshund. You will need a harness and a tracking lead, which must be between 20 and 40 feet long. You also will need access to some wide-open spaces for laying tracks.

What Is Tracking?

Tracking is an organised sport that tests any bred's ability to follow a scent. This is a fun sport for Dachshunds, and for people who like to spend a lot of time training outside. In the UK, tracking is incorporated in Working Trials, which is a discipline that also involves control and agility, and in the advanced stages, manwork (catching and apprehending a "criminal"). Dachshunds have proved to be very successful in this challenging sport.

In the US, tracking is a sport in its own right. To start with, dogs are given a scent and must find a glove. They can't just go straight to the glove, but must follow the scent trail as it has been laid out. Dogs experienced at tracking can go on to do other tracking-related

An agility course requires a dog to manoeuvre through tunnels, jumps, weaving poles, and other obstacles.

work like search and rescue or drug detection.

At the basic level, the scent trail is laid out in an open field and is about 500 metres long with three to five turns in the trail. The trail is aged about two hours. As the levels get tougher, trails get longer with more turns, distracting cross tracks and obstacles like roads, ditches, and woods. They are also aged longer so the scent trail is older and fainter. Any breed can compete in tracking, and this sport is a lot of fun. Tracking people are famous for their willingness to help beginners get into the sport, and Dachshunds typically enjoy this time outdoors with their people.

Titles in organised tracking events include:

- Tracking Dog (TD)
- Tracking Dog Excellent (TDX)
- Variable Surface Tracker (VST)
- Champion Tracker (CT)

WORKING TRIALS

Dachshunds do very well at working trials, as the breed is able to use its natural abilities to perform tasks that will satisfy

its mental and physical needs. Working trials is a competitive discipline in which dogs are assessed on a variety of working skills and abilities. Dogs must progress through levels of increasing difficulty known as "stakes". The stakes are; Companion Dog (CD), Utility Dog (UD), Working Dog (WD), Tracking Dog (TD), and Patrol Dog (PD).

Each stake is comprised of three sections: nosework, agility and control. Nosework tests the dog's ability to follow a scent trail.

Agility, as the name suggests, assesses a dog's physical agility. Canine competitors have to successfully negotiate a number of obstacles, including jumps and scale.

The control section involves some traditional obedience-style exercises, including heelwork, a sendaway and a retrieve.

In Patrol Dog stake, there is an extra section called manwork, in which the dog must successfully apprehend and control a 'criminal'.

Points are awarded for each exercise, and if the dog is awarded enough points, he achieves the title for that stake and is eligible for entry into the next level. The dog must obtain a minimum of 70 percent of the marks available in each section, as well as 80 percent or more of the total marks overall to be awarded the Excellent qualification in each stake e.g. C.Dex, U.Dex, etc. Except for the CD the dog must first gain a Certificate of Merit at an Open Trial to enable him to compete in the relevant Championship Stake.

In the US, there are no working trials. Instead, agility and obedience form competitive sports in their own right and there is an extra discipline of tracking tests. To earn the title Tracking Dog (TD), the dog must pass a tracking test that involves following a scent trail of between 440 and 500 yards (400 and 450 metres) that scent trail was laid 30 minutes and 2 hours earlier. He can then proceed to the Tracking Dog Excellent tracking test to earn the title Tracking Dog Excellent (TDX). At this level, the track will be longer, include more changes of direction and will have been laid for a longer period before the dog is allowed to start following. The next level is the Variable Surface Tracking test, which shows that a dog has demonstrated his ability to follow a scent on a variety of different surfaces, including in an urban setting. A Champion Tracker (CT) is a dog who has earned all three AKC tracking titles.

Unlike obedience and agility titles that require a dog and handler to qualify three times, a Dachshund only needs to compete

Dachshunds can excel at Earthdog trials, which require them to go underground to search out quarry.

one track successfully to earn each title.

FIELD TRIALS

Field trials test your dog's ability to follow a trail, and here is where you'll hear them give voice as they trail the rabbit. In field trials, dogs are run in pairs, or braces, and they are judged on how well they search for and pursue game, accuracy in trailing, obedience to commands, use of voice, and their willingness to follow the rabbit into a burrow. The dogs love this sport, and there's not much training involved.

EARTHDOG TRIALS

Earthdog Trials is a growing sport in the US and has yet to reach the UK.

Dachshunds can earn three different titles in Earthdog competition: Junior Earthdog (JE), Senior Earthdog (SE), and Master Earthdog (ME). The AKC Earthdog Event tests a dog's willingness to follow prey into their den. A cage containing rats is at the end of the tunnel.

The Introduction to Quarry is an instinct test. You might want to try this first to see if your Dachshund has an interest in going to ground. This test is a 10-foot long tunnel with one 90-degree turn.

For the Junior Earthdog title, a dog must qualify at two different tests under two different judges. There is a 30-foot tunnel and three 90-degree turns. There is an entrance at one end, and a quarry area at the other end, with no additional entrances, exits, or dead ends.

To earn the Senior Earthdog title, the dog must have already earned the JE title and must qualify at three different tests under two different judges. In this test there is a 30-foot main tunnel, three 90-degree turns, a secondary exit and a false den. The secondary exit should be approximately 7 feet in length with one 90-degree turn. The false den will be a side tunnel approximately

Whether competing with one or several Dachshunds, it's your responsibility to make sure they're safe at any event.

4 feet in length with no exit. The false den will have a heavily scented simulated litter/bedding area. The entrance to the den is camouflaged by a 4-inch dirt mound providing a steep 45-degree entrance to the den.

If your Dachshund loves going to ground, now's the time to try for the title Master Earthdog. To earn the ME title, the dog must qualify at four different tests under two different judges. The tunnel setup is the same as for the SE, but with the following modifications: the entrance is not readily visible but is blocked with a removable obstruction. A 20-foot scent line leads to the entrance, but an unscented false den entrance is located midway along the scent line. There is an 18-inch section of the tunnel that constricts to a 6-inch passage. There is an obstacle in the tunnel, which is a 6-inch diameter section of PVC pipe, suspended crossways in the tunnel with 9 inches on each side of the pipe's centreline.

For all these tests there is a time limit, and when the dog reaches the quarry, he is expected to "work" the quarry—make every effort to reach it—for a specific amount of time.

CANINE FREESTYLE

Just when you think no one could possibly come up with yet another canine sport, along comes another one! Dancing with dogs is an exciting and invigorating sport that allows you and your dog to kick up your heels, so to speak. In the simplest terms, it is a choreographed performance between a dog and handler that is set to music. This relatively new sport of canine musical freestyle combines obedience and dance to demonstrate teamwork and rapport between dog and handler. Both handler and dog are judged on several parameters. These include:

- Content of routine
- Accuracy
- Overall impression

There are different types of routine that are judged in different classes. Heelwork to Music, as the name suggests, must contain a percnetage of close work, with the dog working in a variety of positions,

When It's Hot Outside

In obedience, the long sits and downs may be in the direct sun. If there is any shade in the ring, most judges will use that area for these exercises, but maybe not. Check it out ahead of time.

Agility is hot and fast, but if you keep your Dachshund comfortable before and after your run, there shouldn't be a problem. If a trial is being run in hot weather, most clubs will have wading pools of water where you can cool your dog off after a run.

such as left of the handler, right, in front, behind, and to the side. Freestyle routines are more flamboyant, as the dog can work at any distance from the handler, and they often include spectacular moves.

In the UK, the sport is recognised by the Kennel Club and competitions are held throughout the year. Competitors begin in starters and work their way up through novice and intermediate to advanced level. There is a competition held annually at Crufts

Their short legs won't win them any applause for drama at Frisbee-throwing contests, but it doesn't mean you and your Dachshund can't enjoy a catch. Keep your throws low to the ground, however; leaping and twisting can hurt your Dachshund's back.

that draws big crowds. If you want to find out more about dancing with dogs, go to the Kennel Club website - www.thekennelclub.org.uk. Alternatively, visit the website of the World Canine Freestyle Organization, Inc. (WCFO) at www.caninefreestyle.co.uk.

SPORTS AND SAFETY

The sport of dogs offers all kinds of competitive events at many different levels. It's great fun to compete with your dog, but keep your best friend's safety in mind, too.

Dachshunds as Therapy Dogs

Dachshunds make good therapy dogs because their size is not threatening. A drawback is that they are a bit hard to reach to pet when a person is in a wheelchair or a bed, but you can easily pick up your dog and hold him for the loving attention of those you are visiting.

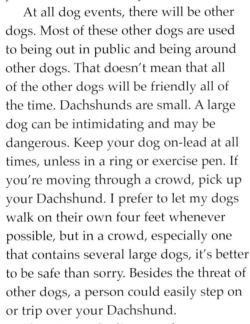

At all dog events, there will be other dogs. Most of these other dogs are used to being out in public and being around other dogs. That doesn't mean that all of the other dogs will be friendly all of the time. Dachshunds are small. A large dog can be intimidating and may be dangerous. Keep your dog on-lead at all times, unless in a ring or exercise pen. If you're moving through a crowd, pick up your Dachshund. I prefer to let my dogs walk on their own four feet whenever possible, but in a crowd, especially one that contains several large dogs, it's better to be safe than sorry. Besides the threat of other dogs, a person could easily step on or trip over your Dachshund.

If you're in obedience and your Dachshund doesn't always hold his stays, and you're afraid he might leave the ring, mention it to the steward before you go in, so they are prepared to block the gate.

Those contact areas on agility equipment are there for a reason: to help prevent injury to your dog. Train your dog to hit the contact areas. I've watched people with very fast dogs bring them to a halt coming off the contact obstacles. Sure, it may cost a second or two in time, but the dog isn't leaping off to a potential injury.

With their loving personalities and convenient size, Dachshunds can make excellent therapy dogs with the proper training.

With any event, remember that your Dachshund is very sensitive to heat, and his short nose and face make it harder for him to cool off. If you're showing in conformation, and you keep your Dachshund cool before and after his appearance in the ring, the heat shouldn't be a problem; but with performance events, if the humidity is 90 percent and the temperature is 85 degrees, you may want to pull your entry.

THERAPY DOGS

If your own tendencies lean more toward couch potato than athlete, maybe therapy work is the niche for you and your Dachshund. Dachshunds are so loving that therapy work is a wonderful choice for them. Visiting a nursing home doesn't require much physical effort, but the emotional rewards can be tremendous. This is a chance for you to share your wonderful dog

with people whose activities have become limited.

There are organisations that register therapy dogs, such as Pets As Therapy. For more information you can visit their website, www.petsastherapy.org.uk. Actually having a registered therapy dog means that your dog has been assessed to check his temperament by accredited assessors. If your dog becomes a registered therapy dog, he will have a special photo ID tag for his collar. The registering agency will need proof that your dog passed the necessary test and that all vaccinations are up to date. The agency may provide insurance coverage for visits, and will offer guidelines for taking your dog to hospitals or other health care facilities.

Your dog may or may not be permitted into a person's lap or onto a bed. Check with the facility manager before you allow either of these behaviours. Older people have more delicate skin, and there may be a concern that the dog's nails will bruise or tear the skin. That's why it's so important to make sure your dog's nails are short and that he is absolutely clean.

ACTIVITIES AT HOME

Dachshunds want to be near you and most will try hard to please you, but if it turns out that you and your Dachshund don't really enjoy any of these activities, don't worry. You can enjoy impromptu games in your own home.

Hide-and-Seek

Almost all dogs enjoy hide-and-seek. Put your Dachshund on a sit-stay (or have a family member hold him). Hide somewhere— maybe just in another room at first, and call your Dachshund. He'll enjoy trying to find you. As your Dachshund gets used to the game, you can hide behind doors or in closets.

You also can play another kind of hide-and-seek with a treat. At first, use a treat that has a very definite odour, like a small cube of cheese. Keep it in your closed hand, but let your Dachshund smell it. Go to a different room and hide the treat. Again, the first few times you may want to hide it in a simple place, maybe even in the middle of the floor, just to give your dog the idea.

Games in the House

Games are interactive fun for both of you - and for other members of the family.

Try these, and then think up some of your own!

Find Dad!

Well, find Dad, or Mum, Aunt Sue, or your son or daughter - anyone your dog sees regularly. Start by sitting down with two people - let's call them Joe and Jane. Jane says "Find Joe!" and Joe shows the dog he has a treat. When the dog comes to eat the treat tell him he's wonderful! Then, Jane holds a treat, and Joe says, "Find Jane!" The clever Dachshund merrily goes to her - and gets a treat. Gradually Joe and Jane get farther apart from each other until they are eventually around the corner from each other.

Soon, one of them can go into another room, and they can send the dog to find each other. They can even send messages to each other via the dog!

Clean The House!

Why not get some help from your Dachshund to clean the house?

If your dog likes to play fetching games, and if you've taught him to 'Drop It', you have a perfect helper. Ask him to pick up a toy, and then clap your hands and have him follow you to a basket or toy storage bin. Then tell him 'Drop It' and give him lots of praise and treats when he drops the toy in the basket. Once he understands the game, you can show him socks you want him to pick up. He'll be better than a housekeeper!

Tricks

You also can teach your dog tricks, like rolling over or giving a high-five. There are several good books out there on how to teach your dog tricks. Clicker training makes it easy to build on those tricks and even create entire routines. Best of all, your Dachshund will love showing off.

Don't really want to do any of this? That's fine. Your Dachshund will be just as happy with regular walks, lots of cuddling, and as many treats as he can beg. The idea is to spend time together and enjoy each other's company.

Your Dachshund may love to preform tricks such as shaking hands, rolling over, or playing dead.

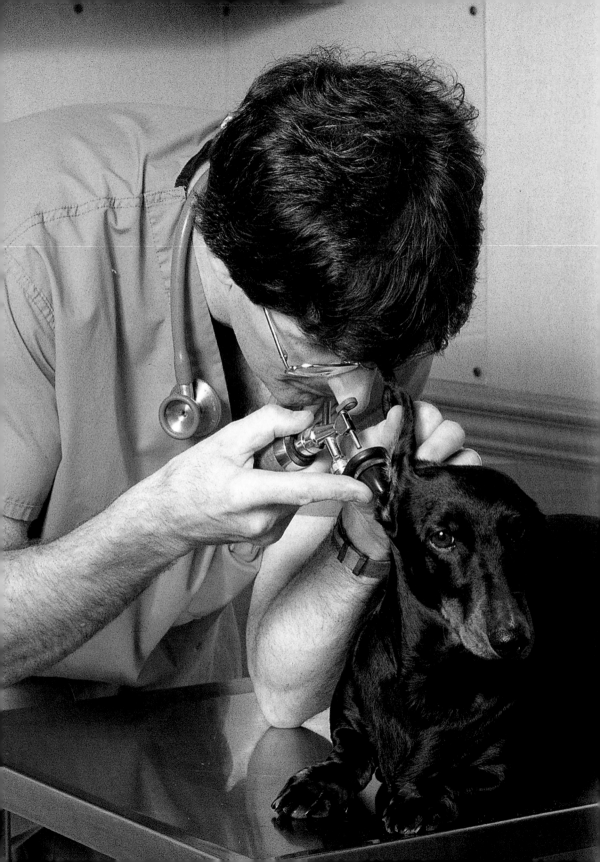

Chapter

8

HEALTH

of Your Dachshund

The health of your Dachshund will be a concern from the day you bring home that cute little puppy until the sad day when you finally say good-bye. It's up to you to provide the best care you can for your dog and to understand some of the issues that your dog will face throughout his life. Depending on your contract with the breeder, there will be a specified window of time for getting a clean bill of health or returning the puppy to the breeder. The time limit may be anywhere from 48 hours to one month, with the shorter time frame more common.

CHOOSING A VETERINARIAN

First, find a veterinarian that you like and feel comfortable with, one who is willing to discuss your dog's health care with you. If possible, find this veterinarian before you get your puppy.

Ask friends who have pets which veterinarian they go to, and why. If they have a complaint about a particular practice, is it legitimate?

Large Practice or Small?

Think about whether you want to take your dog to a large practice with multiple vets, or to a smaller practice. There can be advantages to both. In a small practice, the veterinarian may get to know you and your dog better than if you see different vets on different visits. The disadvantage is that if your veterinarian is on holiday or ill, a veterinarian from a different practice won't know you at all. In an emergency, that vet won't have any background on your pet. With a larger practice, while a particular veterinarian might not really know you, he will have easy access to your pet's entire medical history. Distance may determine which veterinarian you go to. If you've gotten recommendations for more than one practice, you may want the one closest to your home. Or maybe there's a practice where one of the veterinarians has Dachshunds of his own. That may appeal to you. All dogs have health issues particular to their breed, and a veterinarian who is familiar with Dachshunds will be more aware of what to look for when he's

How comfortable you are with the veterinarian, support staff, and facilities is more important than proximity to your home.

examining your Dachshund.

Consider the practice's response to emergencies. Is there someone on call at night and on holidays? Does the staff seem willing to squeeze you in if there's a sudden problem, or do they brush you off? Are the surgery and waiting room clean? Will the veterinarian take the time to explain what he or she is doing?

Be Comfortable With Your Choice

You may not be able to answer all these questions without a visit or two to the surgery, but if anything makes you uncomfortable, find another veterinarian. Even if everything about the practice is perfect, if you aren't happy with the veterinarian for whatever reason, go elsewhere. You want someone who can care for your pet, of course, but you also want someone you are comfortable around who will talk to you about your pet's care and answer your questions. You also want someone who will listen to you. Even the best veterinarian won't know your dog as well as you will. Ideally, you and your veterinarian will be partners, working to keep your dog healthy.

Dachshund puppies are so cute that the veterinary staff will probably pay some extra attention to your puppy before the examination. This will be good for the puppy, as it will give him a pleasant association with the practice, not just the memory of a shot.

The First Visit

If your puppy hasn't received all his shots, this initial visit becomes even more important. Both distemper and parvovirus are often fatal in puppies, so this is not a visit to ignore or postpone.

At this first appointment, if you have any concerns or questions about proper health care, ask your vet. If you are uncomfortable about brushing your puppy's teeth, for example, ask for a demonstration and discuss different methods. Ask about flea and tick protection. Ask if there are any specific health concerns related to your part of the country, such as Lyme disease. Your dog's health will be your responsibility for the next 14 to 16 years, so start off right.

When you bring your puppy home, he should not have any evidence of fleas or ticks and should have been wormed, since most puppies are born with roundworms. Puppies are typically tested and treated for roundworms at two, four, six, and eight weeks. Your breeder should supply the dates and the kind of medicine used.

Depending on the age of your puppy, he may or may not have received his first set of vaccinations. Currently, many veterinarians give the first set of shots at 8 weeks, then 12 weeks, 16 weeks, and then annually after that, although some veterinarians also may recommend shots at 18 to 20 weeks, and then annually. Check with the breeder to see what, if any, shots have been given to your puppy.

Usually, the shots given are combination vaccinations that include protection against distemper, leptospirosis, hepatitis, parvovirus, and also may or may not include parainfluenza.

Also talk to your veterinarian about the effects of vaccinations, and about whether or not annual vaccinations are needed. After your first vaccination, stay at the veterinarian's surgery for a while to see if your Dachshund is going to have a reaction. If he does, the medical staff will be available to quickly counteract the reaction.

If your dog does react to vaccinations, make sure to notify your veterinarian. If he knows this, he might break up the shots for your dog. Splitting up the doses doesn't mean your veterinarian is

Rabies Vaccinations

Rabies does not exist in the UK. However, if you are travelling overseas with your Dachshund you will be required to have your dog vaccinated. Your vet will be able to give you all the information you need.

just trying to get more money from you. It means he is concerned about your dog. Many veterinarians no longer routinely give the Leptospirosis vaccine. Ask your veterinarian about this.

MODERN VACCINE PROTOCOL

The practice of giving every dog every kind of vaccination every year has been challenged in recent years, so that is another thing to talk to your veterinarian about. Tests have shown that almost three-quarters of tested dogs still have a high blood titer against the disease they were vaccinated for, but a high titer doesn't guarantee that they will in fact fight off a disease.

Rather than automatically vaccinating every dog every year, many veterinarians now vaccinate on a case-by-case basis. They might vaccinate show dogs or dogs who travel frequently more

You and your veterinarian should discuss the important and necessary vaccines your Dachshund will need as a puppy and an adult.

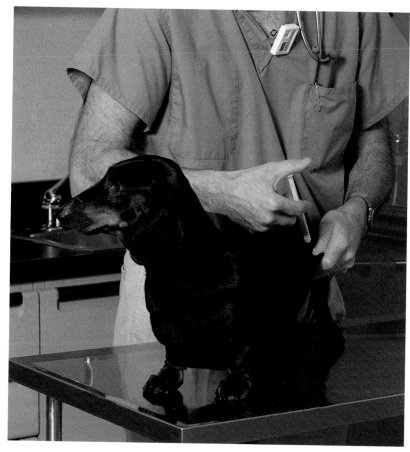

Be sure to vaccinate your dog against dangerous and potentially fatal illnesses such as distemper, and parovirus.

often than older, stay-at-home dogs.

Currently, drug companies are working on longer-lasting vaccinations that would protect for three to four years. Ask your veterinarian about this, as these should soon be available.

Diseases to be Vaccinated Against

Distemper

Distemper is another dangerous disease that has a very low recovery rate. The danger from this very contagious virus is greatest in dogs three to six months of age and in dogs over six years of age. Symptoms include vomiting, diarrhoea, coughing, and fever, and death is the usual outcome.

Parovirus

Parvovirus is another disease that may be fatal, especially if the

Common Sense Care

Never give your dog alcoholic beverages. A drunken dog is not funny; a drunken dog is sick, and it doesn't take much to result in alcohol poisoning, which could lead to death.

symptoms include vomiting and bloody diarrhoea. There may be a fever, and the dog will be lethargic and depressed. Dogs with mild cases of the disease generally recover, but young puppies are very susceptible and generally do not survive. (This is why those early shots are so important.)

Coronavirus

Coronavirus is a highly contagious virus that results in diarrhoea for about a week. The diarrhoea may be orange-tinged and will have a strong odour. The disease is rarely fatal, but the dog may need to be treated for dehydration. Talk to your veterinarian

Dogs that spend any amount of time outdoors are liable to pick up fleas and ticks. Preventive care is a must to keep these parasites under control.

about the need for this shot. A healthy, mostly indoor dog might not need this shot, but it might be advisable for a show dog, or a dog that regularly comes in contact with many other dogs. Since the disease is rarely fatal, you might want to just take your chances.

Canine Hepatitis

Dogs with mild to moderate cases of infectious canine hepatitis generally have a fever and are lethargic. They may be reluctant to move and have abdominal tenderness and pale mucous membranes. The mucous membranes may be bright red, yellow, pale, or have petechiation (small red spots/bruising) depending on the stage or course of the disease. An infected dog can recover anywhere from one to five days after showing symptoms, or the disease may progress to death. In dogs with severe cases, the dog may vomit, have diarrhoea, and develop a cough. Sudden death may result. The disease is spread through faeces and urine.

Leptospirosis

Leptospirosis is a bacteria frequently transmitted through urine, especially that of rats and mice. Symptoms include vomiting, fever, and a reluctance to move. There also may be signs of renal failure. Severe cases can be fatal. If you live in an area where your dog will be exposed to the urine of rats and mice, you might want to make sure your dog is protected against Leptospirosis. Otherwise, this may be a shot you can skip. Consult with your veterinarian.

Rabies

This is not applicable to dogs born in the UK, but it is important if you plan to take your dog overseas. Rabies is a fatal virus that attacks the nervous system and causes encephalitis. Rabies is transmitted in saliva from infected animals. Symptoms include personality changes, fever, aggression, salivation, paralysis, and death.

Other Important Vaccines

Lyme Disease

The deer tick spreads Lyme disease, and symptoms include lethargy, loss of appetite, and lameness. It is treated with antibiotics. Ask your vet if this disease is a problem in your area.

Flea Fighting Tip

Combing your dog with a flea comb also will help trap the unwanted guests. A friend of mine combs her dog at the door whenever he comes inside and has had success in keeping down the flea population.

Allergic Reactions

When you're checking your dog for external parasites, you also should pay attention to his skin. Dogs can be allergic to foods, moulds, and pollens, just like people. Usually, these allergies cause itchy skin. If the discomfort is seasonal, it's probably "something in the air." If it's continuous, it could be the food. If your dog's reaction is not too severe, you may have the time to try different foods, such as foods with rice as the basic grain instead of corn or wheat. If there's a severe reaction, once again, you'll need a trip to the veterinarian. He may want to run some tests, or may suggest a food made of only one ingredient. Then, by gradually adding other foods, you eventually can determine the exact cause of the allergy. It's a lengthy process, but fortunately most dogs don't need to go this route.

If your dog is allergic to flea saliva, he will bite and scratch where a flea has bitten, and may do damage to himself if the irritation drives him to continuous biting and scratching at one spot. Whether or not he is allergic, if he is licking or biting at an area for whatever reason, that area can develop into a hot spot. Hot spots are raw, red, oozy-looking spots that can spread and get infected if not treated. I use a triple antibiotic salve on hot spots, and this seems to clear them up. If a hot spot doesn't get better or continues to get larger, check with your veterinarian.

Bordetella

Vaccination recommendations will depend on where you live, or what you're doing with your dog. Most boarding kennels require a bordetella (kennel cough) vaccination, and that's a good idea if you're travelling a lot, or showing, as kennel cough is highly contagious. Keep in mind that even with a bordetella shot, your dog may still catch kennel cough. There are many varieties, and the vaccine only protects against a few of those. Kennel cough can be treated with antibiotics, and while any disease is cause for concern, kennel cough is not usually serious.

The trend is now moving away from giving every dog every shot, just because the vaccine is available. Some people will even have a blood test done to see if the dog really needs an annual booster. Talk to your veterinarian about what is best for your Dachshund.

EXTERNAL PARASITES

Fleas

Depending on where you live and the time of year you get your puppy, you already may have encountered fleas or ticks. The flea generally seen in and around dogs is the cat flea, which is not native to this continent, but actually originated in Africa. It is getting resistant to many of the flea control products on the market today. Fleas are nasty little critters, and if your dog happens to be allergic to flea saliva, they can make your pet miserable.

Many Dachshunds seem to be especially sensitive to flea bites, so you must control fleas aggressively. They are particularly prevalent during warm, damp weather.

If your dog is scratching and you suspect fleas, turn him over and inspect his stomach, especially toward the back legs where the fur is thinner. Push the hair against the grain. You may see a flea or two scurrying for cover. Or, you may not see a flea at all, but you may notice flecks of flea dirt. If you're not sure if what you're looking at is flea dirt, or just regular dirt, collect a bit on a white piece of paper or paper towel, and wet it. If it turns reddish, it's flea dirt.

If you don't see anything on your dog but still suspect fleas, run a flea comb through your dog's coat. Flea combs have very fine, closely set teeth that can trap fleas. Once you've determined that there are fleas, the war has begun.

There are many different products on the market designed to eliminate fleas, and your veterinarian can help you choose the one best suited for your dog. If your dog is heavily infested, a bath using a flea-fighting shampoo is a good start.

Ticks

Ticks may or may not be a problem in your area. If you take long walks in tall grass or through brush, you are more likely to pick up a tick or two than in a garden. Deer ticks, which are very small, can spread Lyme disease. Ask your vet if this is a concern in your area, as there is a vaccine for Lyme disease.

You can remove ticks gently with tweezers, or put alcohol on them. Never use a cigarette or anything else that will burn. Undoubtedly that would get the tick's attention, but you are also likely to burn your dog. If you don't think you can get the tick off properly, or just don't want to try, have your veterinarian do it for you. The important thing is to check your dog on a routine basis if ticks are a problem in your area and not leave them on your dog. Ticks can be hard to find, so be patient and thorough.

Mites

Mites can cause mange, another skin problem to watch out for. There are two types of mange, both caused by tiny mites: sarcoptic and demodectic. With sarcoptic mange, there is intense itching,

Vacuuming to Curb Fleas

Daily vacuuming is as effective as any spray in keeping the flea population down in the house. You can cut up a flea collar and put it in the vacuum bag to help kill the fleas. Also, change the vacuum bag frequently, or you'll be supporting a flea colony in the bag. Wash your dog's bed frequently, as that is where most of the flea eggs will accumulate.

and with advanced cases, skin lesions and hair loss. It is important to seek veterinary advice as soon as you suspect a case of mange. Treatment usually lasts for three weeks. The dog's bedding also should be thoroughly disinfected or thrown away.

Demodectic mange is passed from the mother to the puppies and affects puppies between the ages of three and ten months. With demodectic mange, you may notice hair loss around the eyes, lips, or on the forelegs. The dog also may lose hair at the tips of the ears. Demodectic mange doesn't cause the itching that sarcoptic mange does and is usually diagnosed from skin scrapings. A special shampoo may be recommended. Demodectic mange, if not widespread on the dog's body, may go away on its own. If it spreads beyond small, localised areas, it may need up to a year of treatment.

INTERNAL PARASITES (WORMS)

Internal parasites can be harder to detect than those living on the surface, and that's why a faecal check once or twice a year is so important. Whipworms, hookworms, and roundworms all can be discovered by a faecal check. Heartworms require a blood test, and tapeworm segments are usually evident in the stool and can be seen with the naked eye.

Internal parasites such as heartworms can be very dangerous, even fatal, to your dog.

Puppies can get worms from their mother's milk, but are easily treated as long as you take your puppy for his first vet checkup promptly.

Tapeworms

Tapeworms are the least harmful of the worms that may infest your dog. Your Dachshund can acquire tapeworms from swallowing a flea, so controlling the flea population is one of the best ways to prevent tapeworms in your dog. Tapeworm segments are visible in the stool and will look like small grains of rice. Check your dog's stool periodically for evidence of tapeworms.

Hookworms

Hookworm eggs are passed in the faeces and can live in the soil. They also may be passed from a bitch to her puppies. Instead of maturing, larvae may live in the bitch and then pass to the puppies through the mammary glands. Hookworms feed on the blood of their host and can cause fatal anaemia in puppies.

Roundworms

Roundworms are the most common worms that can affect your dog. They contaminate the soil and the eggs are very resistant to adverse conditions. They are able to remain in soil for years. Most puppies are born with these worms because the larvae are able to live in an intermediate host, in this case the bitch, but not infect her. This is why it is necessary to worm young puppies.

Whipworms

Whipworms can cause deep inflammation of the colon. If your dog has periodic bouts of diarrhoea with mucus and blood, he may have whipworms. Again, contaminated soil is to blame. Protect your dog from worms with periodic faecal checks and use the medicine your veterinarian prescribes to get rid of them.

Heartworms

Found throughout the United States, they are potentially the most dangerous internal parasites. Fortunately, this parasite is not usually found in the UK. Mosquitoes transmit the disease when they suck blood from an infected dog and then bite a healthy dog, thereby depositing larvae. The larvae grow inside the healthy dog, migrating through the dogs tissues into the bloodstream, and eventually into the dog's heart. The larvae grow into adult worms. Preventative medications are available and are highly recommended in the US. If you are travelling with your Dachshund to any area where heartworm is prevalent, it is imperative that

Your Dachshund's big, beautiful eyes are particularly prone to irritants and other problems.

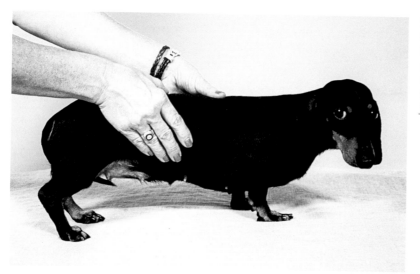

The Dachshund's long spine and short legs make him prone to intervertebral disc degeneration. Your veterinarian should know to check your dog's spine for this problem.

you consult with your vet for advice on a suitable preventative treatment before you go.

DISEASES COMMON TO DACHSHUNDS

Eye Problems

Because he stands low to the ground, a Dachshund's eyes are more vulnerable to dirt, dust, grass, and other irritants. Dachshunds also may be susceptible to entropion, a condition in which the eyelashes grow inward, scratching the eye. This can be corrected by surgery.

Trichiasis is a similar problem, where otherwise normal eyelashes turn inward, irritating the cornea. Again, surgery can be performed to correct the problem.

Progressive retinal atrophy (PRA) is another eye condition affecting Dachshunds that can lead to blindness. Ask your breeder if she tests her breeding stock for this disease. PRA generally strikes older dogs. There is no treatment, and a dog's symptoms will progress over time from vision loss at night to total blindness.

Back Problems

Dachshunds are prone to intervertebral disc degeneration, which is a degeneration of the cushioning discs between the vertebrae of the spinal cord. When a disc ruptures, this puts pressure on the nerves and can result in pain and/or lameness or paralysis. While jumping will not cause the problem, it may aggravate it. Keeping your dog at a proper weight and in good muscle tone will help. If a disc does rupture, anti-inflammatories and rest may be enough to get your dog back to normal. In severe cases, surgery may be required.

Your Dachshund also may injure a disc by just being a dog. Dachshunds are bold little dogs who may think nothing of launching from the sofa or your bed. It's up to you to make sure your Dachshund doesn't do this. Lift your Dachshund down from the furniture. Yes, he's willing to jump down, but with those short legs and that long back, he could injure himself. Pay attention to how you pick up your dog as well, and don't let his hindquarters dangle in space. Make sure you support the entire dog when you lift or carry him.

Playing Frisbee with your Dachshund is probably not a good idea either, because leaping and twisting can result in a back injury. Just throw a ball and let him run straight after it. Again, keeping your dog at the right weight will help prevent back strain. The more your dog weighs, the harder it is on his skeleton.

Raising puppies is expensive and time consuming, and unless you plan for them very carefully, it's best to spay or neuter your dogs and leave the breeding to professionals.

Spondylosis deformans is a degenerative condition of the spine. Bony spurs form around the edges of the vertebral end plates, and these spurs may bridge, or almost bridge, the spaces between vertebral discs. The condition causes stiffness and back pain, and the dog also may be lame. X-rays will determine if this is the problem, and a veterinarian generally will prescribe nonsteroidal anti-inflammatory drugs to treat the pain.

Epilepsy

Epilepsy is another condition that can affect Dachshunds, and currently there is no way to genetically test for this problem. In many cases, the seizures can be controlled with medication.

A seizure may or may not be indicative of epilepsy. To be defined as epilepsy, many veterinarians say there needs to be recurrent seizures with no other disease detected. Sometimes a dog will have an isolated seizure and never have another one. Although the seizure itself is not likely to hurt the dog unless he bumps into or falls against something, watching a seizure can be frightening. Be calm until the seizure is over and then call your veterinarian for his advice. Most likely he'll ask you to describe the seizure and tell you to keep watching your dog. If it makes you feel better, ask for an appointment for a checkup for your dog.

During a seizure, a dog may have muscle spasms, paddle with his legs, salivate, urinate, defecate, vomit, or any combination of these things. A dog having a partial seizure may try to crawl to you. Reassurance and love may shorten the seizure. Be careful, though; if your dog is having a seizure, because sometimes dogs having a seizure may snap or bite.

There is currently no way to genetically test for epilepsy, and if your dog only has the occasional seizure, there likely will be no treatment. If seizures are frequent, your veterinarian may prescribe an anticonvulsant. Acupuncture also may be useful in controlling seizures.

Teeth and Gum Problems

The teeth are easy to ignore, but teeth and gum problems can lead to more serious problems as bacteria are produced and circulated throughout the dog. See Chapter 5 to learn ways to brush your dog's teeth and help prevent dental problems. If you suspect a problem, have your veterinarian examine your Dachshund's teeth.

Watching Your Dog's Weight After Being Fixed

There shouldn't be much weight gain in a spayed or neutered animal if their exercise level doesn't change. None of my females ever gained any weight after being spayed, but my male did, in fact, gain a bit. Cutting his food from a cup a day to three-quarters of a cup a day brought him back to his ideal weight.

When to Call the Vet

A dog's normal temperature is between 100° and 102°F (37.8 and 38.9°C), with a heart rate of 80 to 140 beats per minute. If the temperature goes above 104° (40°C), or below 100°F, call the veterinarian. If the dog is bleeding and the blood is spurting, or can't be stopped by pressure, call the veterinarian.

Taking your Dachshund's temperature may assist your veterinarian in treating an emergency or routine medical situation.

Obesity

Obesity shouldn't be a problem in dogs because they have people to control their food intake. Unfortunately, it's all too easy to give in to those pleading eyes and slip the dog a piece of cheese or the leftover pizza crust. Or sometimes people think kibble looks unappealing, and that adding a bit of meat and gravy will make it taste better. Or, while training, they forget that all those food rewards also add calories.

Once a dog gets fat, the extra weight affects his health. Added weight can lead to added stress on that long spine, heart problems, and diabetes. A fat dog also has trouble exercising, so he may gain even more weight.

If you can't feel your dog's ribs when you run your hands over his sides, he's too fat.

Hyperthyroidism

Hyperthyroidism in dogs is usually caused by a tumour on the thyroid. Symptoms include weight loss, increased appetite, heat intolerance, restless behaviour, frequent defecation with only partially formed stools, increased drinking, and increased urinating. Treatment is done through surgery, and, if the tumour is cancerous and has spread, radioiodine and chemotherapy.

Hypothyroidism

Dachshunds are one of the breeds at increased risk for hypothyroidism. The problem is usually seen between 4 and 10 years of age. Symptoms include hair loss, usually at the base of the tail, ears and lower back, a dry coat, and flaky, oily skin. The dog may be lethargic, more sensitive to cold, and may gain weight. In severe cases there also may be muscle weakness. The condition is treated with a replacement hormone, which may be administered as a pill, or by injection or IV.

Diabetes

Diabetes is another disease frequently seen in Dachshunds. The onset of the disease is usually between 4 and 14 years, with the peak between 7 and 9 years. Females are more likely to get diabetes than males. Increased drinking and urinating are the most obvious symptoms. In fact, diabetes is commonly diagnosed when a previously housetrained dog starts having accidents in the house. You may notice acetone on your dog's breath; it smells like nail polish remover. In advanced cases of diabetes the dog may be lethargic, dehydrated, and may vomit or have diarrhoea. Injections of insulin are administered to treat diabetes.

Cancer

Cancer is one of the scariest words in the English language, but many cancers, if caught in time, can be treated. Some are more treatable than others, which is why you never should wait if you suspect a problem. Many surface tumours, for example, are easily removed when they are small. Testicular cancer is another form that is usually treated successfully. Some cancers may respond to chemotherapy or radiation treatments, and if they cannot be cured, at least they may be put into remission, giving you more time with

If Your Dog is Poisoned

If you suspect poisoning, don't wait! Call the vet to let her know you're on the way. If you know what your dog ate, you can induce vomiting by administering hydrogen peroxide, but don't encourage vomiting if the substance is unknown. Caustic products, such as many household cleaners, will cause more damage when the dog vomits.

Putting a Muzzle on Your Dog

To properly apply a muzzle of gauze (or rope, or a lead if necessary), make a loop by tying a half-knot in the gauze. Place the loop over the dog's muzzle with the half-knot on top. It probably will be easier to do if you are behind the dog and also will lessen the chance of a bite. Tighten the knot, and bring the ends of gauze under the muzzle. Make another half knot, then bring the ends up behind the dog's ears and tie a bow, or other quick release knot. Now you can examine or transport your Dachshund without fear of being bitten. If your dog is having trouble breathing, don't use a muzzle, which may restrict his efforts to breathe. Instead, try to restrain your dog with a blanket or some other kind of padding that extends around his head and beyond his nose several inches. This will not totally eliminate the chance of a bite, but it will help to diminish it.

Common Toxins Indoors and Out

Sharing a fenced garden with your Dachshund is much more fun than just taking him for walks, but remember, there can be dangers in your own garden. Tomato plant stems and leaves and rhubarb leaves are poisonous. Ask your veterinarian or the people at the garden centre which plants might be toxic to a dog. This doesn't mean that you can't have a garden as well as a dog. For instance, the bulbs of many plants are poisonous, but even if your Dachshund has a passion for digging, a small fence can protect both the flowers and your dog.

your Dachshund.

Groom your dog regularly, and make it a habit to run your hands over his body so that you notice any unusual lump, bump, or sore. If the injury doesn't get better or a lump is growing, make an appointment with your veterinarian. Don't wait and allow for the possibility that the cancer will spread.

SPAYING AND NEUTERING

Between six months and two years of age, besides finishing off the growth period, your dog will become sexually mature. Spaying or neutering can eliminate some of the manifestations of sexual maturity, and certainly this is the best approach if you are not seriously committed to showing or breeding.

As your male matures, he will start "lifting his leg" more and more frequently on walks, marking his territory and announcing his presence to other dogs. He may start marking in the house, as well, which can be a very hard habit to break. He may or may not become more aggressive toward other males. He will certainly become more interested in females. If he is around a female in season, he will pay less attention, if any, to you. If he were to ever get loose, he would be more apt to stray further from home than a neutered male.

If you have a female, you can expect her to come in season sometime between six months and a year of age, and then every six to eight months after that. Ask your breeder what the females are like in her line, as there can be some variation. A bitch is in season for about 21 days, although she is only receptive to a male for 3 to 5 of those days.

The amount of discharge can vary, and how clean the bitch is can also make a difference in how much cleaning up you do. You may want to confine your dog to a room without carpeting while

she is in season. If you have a fenced garden and plan to put her out unattended, make sure the fence is solid and high enough to prevent any wandering males from jumping in. Keep an eye on her. Don't just put her out and forget her. If you are walking her, keep a good grip on the lead and keep your eye out for romantic males. If you own more than one dog and one is an intact male, you just might want to board the bitch, rather than deal with trying to keep her separated from the male in the house. Males can be very persistent and frequently vocal, and three weeks can be a long time.

Besides the benefits of no unwanted litters, spaying a female before her first heat lowers the chance of mammary tumours. After the first heat, there is not much difference in the incidence of these tumours, but spaying does end the chance of pyometra and other reproductive infections as well as the twice-yearly "season." Intact males may be susceptible to prostatic hypertrophy, which is a benign enlargement of the prostate. Neutering prevents prostate problems and may curb aggression and end marking in the house.

On this last point, if you have had a male who persists in lifting his leg against any and all furniture, it is a real relief when he stops. I showed my male until he was about four, and then considered neutering, but was told that at his age, his behaviour patterns were set and neutering would probably not change his habit of marking. I left him alone, going through rolls and rolls of paper towels and bottles and bottles of white vinegar. Then I decided to purchase a puppy bitch to show. I wanted no accidental litters and didn't want the hassle of keeping them separated or boarding one or the other when the bitch came in season. Griffin was neutered. He hasn't marked since. This might not be true for everyone, but it is definitely worth a try.

CONSIDERING BREEDING

If you bought your puppy as a pet, the breeder probably gave you a limited registration and may

Household Poisons

Almost everyone knows that antifreeze can be deadly, and you'd never let your dog drink bleach, but furniture polish, shoe polish, boric acid, deodorants, detergents, and disinfectants are also harmful and should be kept away from your dog.

Dachshund puppies may be adorable, but spaying or neutering your pet is a good idea to prevent any unexpected "additions" to your family.

Knowing some first-aid techniques may save your dog's life in an emergency.

have made spaying or neutering a requirement of the purchase. If, however, the breeder sees promise in the dog and agrees that the quality is there for breeding, be aware that breeding is not something to be undertaken lightly. For starters, there's the stud fee and the cost of shipping your bitch to the male. If you decide on chilled or frozen semen, there's expense involved in gathering, shipping, and inseminating. With these last methods, you'll need daily testing to determine when your female is ready to be bred. There'll be testing for brucellosis, as well as for any hereditary problems. There's the cost of an ultrasound to determine the

number of puppies. You'll need to buy or build a whelping box. The female may need a caesarian section. Some or all of the puppies could die of various causes. The mother could die, leaving you with an orphan litter to feed and clean every two hours. If no one wants the puppies, they'll be your responsibility until you do find them a home, and that means vaccinations, worming, crate training, and the beginning of housetraining.

Breeding is not for the faint of heart. If you are not seriously committed to raising and breeding Dachshunds, and just want another pet, go back to your breeder and buy another one. It will be a lot less work and you'll be much happier.

FIRST AID FOR YOUR DACHSHUND

Dachshunds are generally healthy, but there are things to watch for in any dog. Any problem that persists longer than 24 hours is reason to call your vet. Also, any problem that worsens over several hours, or produces loss of appetite, weakness, or fever needs prompt medical attention. If your dog has a mild case of diarrhoea or vomits once or twice, stop all food for a day and give only water for 24 hours. You may want to feed cooked ground meat with rice for a day or two afterward. If there are frequent bouts of vomiting or diarrhoea, or if it continues for more than 24 hours, call the veterinarian.

There are probably hundreds of products that may be considered poisonous to your dog, but many can be avoided just by using common sense, and many products will probably never be ingested in large enough amounts to harm your pet. For instance, apple seeds contain cyanide. The odds are against your Dachshund ever eating massive quantities of apple seeds. If you are sharing your apple with your Dachshund and he eats a seed or two, don't panic. He should

Use Proper Medications

Buffered aspirin is an appropriate pain or fever reducer at the correct dosage, but always check with your veterinarian before use.

If something is lodged in your dog's mouth, you may need a flashlight to get a better look.

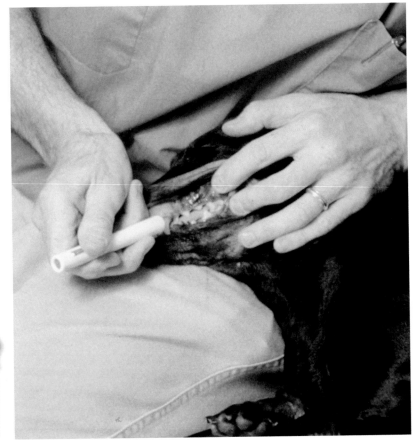

Rehydrating Your Dog

If your dog has been vomiting or has had diarrhoea, he may be dehydrated. Your veterinarian may suggest rehydration fluids. My experience is that your dog won't like it. Try it, but don't be surprised if your dog turns up his nose. My dogs will eat ice cubes in any weather, so I give those. Chicken or beef stock may also tempt them, and the salty taste may encourage them to head for the water bowl as well. Water drained from a can of tuna may flavour a bowl of water enough to encourage your dog to drink.

be fine.

The following first-aid information might make you think twice about even having a dog, but with luck, you won't ever have to worry about any of the problems described below. It's just good to know that there are first-aid measures you can take to help your pet if something ever does happen. First aid courses are available and can help you understand just what you can do to help your pet until you can reach the veterinarian.

Taking Your Dog's Pulse

First, learn to take your dog's pulse. The femoral artery is probably the easiest to find. It's on the upper rear leg, near where the leg joins the body. Find the top bone of the rear leg, which is the femur. Move forward just a bit and you should be able to feel the artery. You might want to ask your vet to help you find it the first time. Find it before you need it, when you and the dog are both calm.

Then, when there's an emergency, you'll be able to find it quickly without panicking.

The normal pulse rate for a dog is between 80 to 140 beats per minute, and the smaller the dog, the higher the number. If you're having your veterinarian show you how to take your dog's pulse, see what your dog's normal range is at the same time, then if there's a problem you'll have a number to use for comparison.

Choking

If your dog is choking on something, use the handle of a screwdriver between the back teeth to keep his mouth open and prevent the dog from biting as you check out his throat and mouth. If you can see the object causing the problem, use your fingers or a pair of needle-nosed pliers to remove it. If you can't reach it, hold your dog upside down by the hind legs and shake him. If that doesn't work, apply forceful, sudden pressure to the abdomen at the edge of the breastbone. (Use your fist. Think Heimlich manoeuvre.)

Staying Calm in an Emergency

In case of a major emergency, such as a dogfight, or if your dog is hit by a car, it is natural to panic, but you need to stay calm for the sake of your dog. In spite of the voice in your head telling you to hurry, slow down and take a moment to think about what your best course of action should be. All too often, improper handling on the spur of the moment can result in further injury to the dog and possible injury to you.

When a dog is hurt, frightened, or in pain, he is apt to snap blindly at any touch, even yours. A muzzle will protect you and make it easier to treat and transport your dog. You might consider buying a nylon muzzle from a pet supply store or catalogue, or you can use a length of gauze from the roll in the first-aid kit.

The best way to transport an injured animal is on a blanket or a board, especially if any spinal cord injury is suspected. Get help, if possible, and try to shift the dog all at once to the blanket or board. Try to move him as little as possible. Call your veterinarian. Give him a brief description of your dog's injuries and tell him you are on the way. Although you may feel calling the veterinary surgery is wasting time, your call gives the staff the time they need to prepare for the emergency. Take the time to call ahead.

Better Safe Than Sorry

Generally, a visit to the veterinarian is needed for any problem (vomiting, diarrhoea, fever, lack of appetite, weakness) that lasts 24 hours or more. The longer you have your Dachshund, the better you'll be able to tell whether a stomach upset just requires some rest and a bland diet to correct it, or whether you need the veterinarian. When in doubt, make the appointment. You'll feel better knowing just what the problem is, and when it comes to your Dachshund's health, it really is better to be safe than sorry.

Acupuncture can be particularly helpful for easing pain and promoting healing.

Injury Checklist

When your dog has been injured, there may be cuts and lacerations. These may produce a lot of blood and look messy, but they are probably the least of your concerns.

In order of importance, check:

1. *Airway/Breathing:* Is the air passage clear? Is breathing laboured?
2. *Circulation:* Is the dog in shock? Is there significant blood loss?
3. *Neurologic:* Has a head, neck or back injury likely occurred?
4. *Orthopaedic:* Do you suspect broken bones?
5. *Ocular:* Do you suspect or detect any significant eye injuries?

Report your findings or suspicions to your veterinarian when you call.

Administering CPR

Make sure there's nothing in your dog's mouth, nose, or throat that is choking him or blocking the airway. If he isn't breathing, you'll need to perform artificial respiration. If you've rescued your Dachshund from a pool, hold him upside down by his hind legs for about 30 seconds to allow fluid to drain from his lungs and mouth before you attempt artificial respiration.

Otherwise, place your dog on his side with his neck extended. Hold the dog's muzzle closed and place your mouth over the dog's nose. Slowly blow air into the dog's nose so that his chest expands. You may also have to administer CPR (Cardio-Pulmonary Resuscitation). Place your dog on his left side and place your thumb on one side of the chest and your fingers on the other side. Compress the chest by squeezing. Do 100 compressions per minute, stopping every 30 seconds to see if the dog is breathing on his own.

Signs of Shock

Now, what about circulation? Is your dog in shock? If your dog has been in a serious fight or has been hit by a car, chances are he'll be in shock. Check the colour of his gums, lips and eyelids. If they are pale, that's a sign of shock. He may feel cool to the touch, especially his legs. See if his temperature is down. His breathing may be shallow and irregular. Check his pulse. It may be fast, irregular and faint. Wrap him in a blanket, or, if you don't have one, a jacket or coat, or even newspapers; anything to keep him warm. Do not use a heat lamp or anything hot close to the body. Because he will likely be unconscious and his circulation will be poor, this could result in burns. Keep him in a horizontal position. A Boy Scout I knew learned a handy phrase in his first-aid course that can also be applied to dogs, "If the head is pale, elevate the tail." There's no need for a huge elevation of the hindquarters, but at least maintain the horizontal position.

Has there been significant blood loss? If so, try to find any external wounds that may need a pressure bandage. If you don't have a bandage, use a towel, or if necessary, your hand. A tourniquet on a leg should only be used as a last resort. A tourniquet stops the blood, which means that all the tissue below the tourniquet will start to die. Use a tourniquet only if you are sure that without it your pet will die. Tighten it only enough to stop the bleeding and get your dog to the veterinarian immediately.

Uses For Aloe Vera

Aloe vera can provide temporary relief for hot spots, bites, and many other skin irritations. Besides being nontoxic, Aloe vera is also bitter so it may discourage licking, which can slow healing.

If your Dachshund has suffered a head, back, or neck injury, try not to move him any more than necessary. Slide him onto a board, a piece of cardboard, or a blanket all at once. Use gauze strips to hold him in place and again, get to your veterinarian.

Do you suspect broken bones? There are all kinds of materials you can use to make a splint for a broken leg. Just remember that the splint should extend beyond the joints on either side of the break. Protect the

If Your Dog Is Lost

No matter what method or methods you use for identification, if your dog should become lost, don't rely on tags, tattoos, or microchips to get your dog back. Be aggressive. Make up posters of your dog. If you've got a scanner, a printer, and a computer, you can make your own posters, complete with picture. Otherwise, have the local copy shop make them for you. A sharp black and white image may be better than a colour picture that doesn't clearly show your dog.

Keep a good photo of your dog on hand in case of emergency. Try to get a picture that shows the dog clearly. Your Dachshund may look adorable curled up in a ball amongst the sofa cushions, but will that adorable pose help to bring him home? The next time you've got the camera out for a holiday or birthday, take a few snaps of your dog. If you've got a black Dachshund, try to take a picture of him against a light background. If your Dachshund is red, find a dark background.

Lost Dog To-Do List

- Take the best picture you have and put it on the poster, along with your phone number. Mention the general area where the dog was lost, for instance, in the vicinity of Green Park, or between Maple and Elm Streets. State the dog's sex. Mention age. It may be more helpful to say "puppy" or "older dog with grey muzzle" than to say a specific age. If the dog is wearing a collar, mention that, as well as the collar's colour. If your photo is in black and white, list the colour or colours of your dog. If your Dachshund is red, you might want to say "brown" on the poster. Remember, not everyone knows that the official name of the Dachshund's colour is red. Offer a reward, but don't specify the amount on the poster.

- Go door to door and ask your immediate neighbours to keep an eye out for your dog. Leave them a poster. Put posters on area bulletin boards, in veterinarian's surgeries, and at local shops. Recruit children. They probably cover more territory on foot than the adults in your neighbourhood, and they may be more apt to notice a dog. Don't encourage children to actually try to catch your dog. Ask them to come to you and lead you to the dog, or to tell their parents and have them call you. A lost dog is frequently a frightened dog, and you don't want him chased further away. You also don't want to run the risk of your dog biting someone out of fear.

- Call area veterinary hospitals. There's a chance your dog could have been hit by a car and taken to a veterinarian's. Call again.

- Check with your local animal shelter. Go in person and look at the dogs. Don't rely on phone calls and don't rely on having someone at a shelter call you. Leave your name and phone number, of course, but also check in person. Notes can be lost, and shelter personnel may change. The person you talk to may not know what a Dachshund is, especially if you have a wirehair or a longhair. They may have seen your dog and thought it was a mixed breed. Go look at the dogs who have been picked up as strays. Go look at least every other day. Show the staff pictures of your dog.

- If there's another shelter 20 or 30 miles away, visit it, too. Dogs, even Dachshunds, can travel amazing distances. Also, if someone picked up your dog and dropped him off again, or lost him, he could end up farther away.

- Run an ad in the Lost and Found column of your local newspaper. Ask your area radio stations to announce it. Many newspapers and radio stations are happy to run these kinds of public service announcements at no charge.

- Notify your breeder. Check with Dachshund rescue. Other Dachshund people can be a helpful resource and if they see a stray Dachshund, can help you get him back. If your area has a local breed club, let them know, too. Dog people are generally eager to help other dog people, and they may be more likely to know what a coated Dachshund looks like.

leg with some padding if you are using sticks or pieces of wood as a splint. Or, you can use a magazine or newspaper for the splint, tying it on with gauze or using vet wrap, or even a nylon or knee sock. If pieces of bone are protruding, don't try to push them back. Cover with a gauze pad and stabilise the area as well as possible.

If there's a puncture wound or other type of injury that penetrates into the chest cavity, try to make it airtight with bandages or plastic wrap. You want it airtight, but not so tight as to hinder breathing. If whatever made the wound is still in it, leave it there for your veterinarian to remove. Use bandages to stabilise the object, if necessary, so it doesn't do any more damage.

Did your Dachshund's eyes escape injury? If the eyelid is bleeding, you may use a gauze pad and gently hold it in place, but remember the word gently. Too much pressure could cause even more damage. If the blood is inside the eyeball, just get to the veterinarian and don't attempt anything yourself. If your

Keep a well-stocked first-aid kit on hand in case of an emergency.

Dachshund's eye has actually popped out of the socket, keep it moist and get to the veterinarian immediately. Use artificial tears, contact lens solution, plain water, cod liver oil, or olive oil. Applying the moisturiser every 15 or 20 minutes should be enough.

With time and practice, you will not panic over minor problems, but will learn when you can wait and when you need to make an emergency visit to the veterinarian's surgery. When in doubt, always call your veterinarian. He can offer the help and reassurance you need. I'd rather pay for an unnecessary surgery visit than ignore something and be sorry later.

A First-Aid Kit

Whether you have a separate first-aid kit for your dog or just keep supplies in a bathroom drawer, there are some basic items you should have on hand in case of emergencies. If you travel frequently with your dog, keep a box of the basics in your car, too. Label the boxes expressly for this purpose, and check the expiration dates on the products occasionally to be sure they're active.

- Syrup of ipecac—give by mouth to induce vomiting
- Activated charcoal—give by mouth if your dog has swallowed something poisonous
- Hydrogen peroxide—to cleanse wounds; this can also induce vomiting
- Gauze rolls or pads
- Adhesive tape
- Cotton balls
- Safety scissors
- Artificial tears—for eye irritation
- Haemostats and/or tweezers
- Digital thermometer
- Syringes (3, 6, and 12 cc)—to administer medication
- Children's Benadryl—for allergic reactions, give 1 milligram per pound
- Children's aspirin or buffered asprin—for fever or pain. Give one tablet per 10 to 15 pounds of body weight.
- Antibiotic ointment—topical for infected wounds
- Hydrocortisone ointment—topical for insect bites or rashes
- Index card with your vet's phone number and the number of the local emergency clinic
- A veterinary first-aid manual
- You might also want some rubber gloves and a roll of vet wrap. This is good for holding bandages or splints in place and it doesn't stick to your dog's fur.

Holistic First-Aid Kit

Should you want to have some alternatives around to handle common problems and emergencies, here are some suggestions from holistic veterinarian Jean Hofve, DVM:

- Cayenne pepper—apply to wounds to help stop bleeding
- Calendula gel—topical for wound healing
- Arnica gel—topical for sprains, strains, bruises

- Comfrey ointment—topical for wound healing
- Rescue Remedy—the Bach Flower remedy all-purpose liquid that's effective for stress or shock

GIVING YOUR DOG MEDICINE

There may be times when your veterinarian will prescribe some form of medication for your Dachshund. Usually, this will be in pill form. If it's an antibiotic, make sure you give it all, even if your dog seems to be better. You want to make sure that an infection is taken care of and doesn't have a chance to flare up again.

Pills are probably the easiest form of medicine to give a Dachshund. Most Dachshunds are chowhounds. Many will gulp down a pill all by itself, or if it's just lying on top of their food. Otherwise, a bit of food around the pill will make it acceptable. With Dachshunds, this can be just about anything. You can use a spoonful of yogurt, a dab of peanut butter, some cream cheese, a bite of hot dog, some tinned dog food, almost anything that your dog will eat quickly, taking the pill with it.

Liquids are a bit harder, unless they have a good flavour and can be mixed with the dog's food. If that doesn't work, pull the dog's lower lip out on the side, making a little pocket into which you can pour the liquid. Then quickly close the dog's mouth and gently stroke his throat until he swallows. Having a helper to hold the dog might be a good idea.

When I've had to put drops and ointment into my dog's eye, I've held him between my legs, and approached the eye from behind. It's not too hard to gently hold open the eye a bit and squeeze in drops or ointment. With ointments, I then close the eye tightly so that the salve will melt and it won't just stick to the eyelashes.

ALTERNATIVE TREATMENTS

More and more veterinary practices are going beyond the bounds of traditional medicine to offer you and your pet as many treatment options as possible. Here are some of them.

Acupuncture

Acupuncture has been practiced on humans in China for more than 4,500 years, and on animals for about 2,000 years. Using hair-fine needles, an acupuncturist stimulates appropriate acupoints to

If you need to give your Dachshund a pill, hide it in some food—he likely will gulp it down without even noticing.

help with healing. Acupoints are tiny areas on the skin that contain relatively concentrated levels of nerve endings, lymphatics, and blood vessels. Acupoints can be identified by their lower electrical resistance, and are usually located in small palpable depressions detectable by trained acupuncturists.

Studies have shown that acupuncture can increase blood flow, lower heart rate, and improve immune function. Acupuncture also stimulates the release of certain neurotransmitters like endorphins, the body's natural painkillers, and smaller amounts of cortisol, an anti-inflammatory steroid.

Acupuncture is commonly used for treating chronic conditions like arthritis and allergies, and to relieve pain and inflammation. Epilepsy may also be helped by acupuncture. Lisa Goldstein, DVM, says that in traditional Chinese medicine acupuncture would be about 20 percent of the treatment, and 80 percent would be herbs, but in this country, people tend to focus more on the acupuncture alone.

Using both acupuncture and herbs, she treated her dog for epilepsy, starting with one treatment a week for three weeks and then once a month for three months, then once every six months, then not at all.

Goldstein says that acupuncture can help speed healing, especially after back surgery. With acupuncture, less pain medicine is needed and the improved blood flow aids healing. She has used it on Dachshunds to help with allergies and skin conditions. Acupuncture can also be used to treat the side effects of cancer, like pain and nausea.

She notes that there are specific "alarm points" that may help indicate what is wrong with an animal. For example, there may be no response when you stimulate the alarm point, but if there is a problem with a specific organ, stimulating the alarm point may provoke a reaction from the animal. A dog may try to bite. Goldstein uses acupuncture to complement Western medicine. She does blood tests and makes her diagnosis based on Western medicine, and then uses the acupuncture to help ease pain and hasten healing. She also encourages her clients to use acupressure points at home in between acupuncture treatments.

Acupuncture Info

If you want to learn more about acupuncture, or want to find a veterinarian in your area who practices acupuncture, www.abva.co.uk for the British Veterinary Acupuncturists.

Homeopathy

Homeopathy is based on the theory that like heals like. A substance is diluted in several stages so that is it safe and free from side effects, yet is still powerful enough to act as a healing

A combination of traditional and alternative medicine may be used to keep your Dachshund healthy.

agent. A rough estimate of more than 3,000 homeopathic remedies are in use. These come in tablets, powders, granules, liquids, and ointments. While the idea may be hard to grasp, it becomes a bit clearer when you realise that, as Goldstein points out, vaccines work the same way.

Herbs

Herbal medicines overall may be gentler and safer when properly administered than extracts or synthetic compounds. This does not mean you should give your dog herbal tablets. Consult with a veterinarian who understands the correct way to use herbs to help heal.

Another aspect of Chinese medicine is the use of certain foods as treatments. An example is using salty foods, such as kelp and seaweed, to soften hardened tissue. This may help with muscle spasms and enlarged lymph glands.

Bach Flower Remedies

Bach flower remedies are often mentioned along with herbal and homeopathic methods. There are 38 single remedies meant to treat emotional problems, such as fear of noise, or shyness. Rescue Remedy, which is a mixture of five of the single remedies, is effective in cases of shock, collapse, and trauma. Many holistic veterinarians will suggest Rescue Remedy as a part of your dog's first-aid kit. Check your local health food store for this product.

Massage

Massage can be a wonderful way to relax your dog, as well as a pleasant way for the two of you to bond. Linda Tellington-Jones developed the Tellington T-touch method of massage in which repeated massaging movements are said to generate specific brain wave patterns that can help an animal that is suffering from anxiety, especially following injuries or surgery. Healing takes place more rapidly when the animal is calm.

Even if your dog is not suffering from an injury, or any form of anxiety, a massage can soothe tired muscles and just plain feel good. It's a terrific way to relax your dog and strengthen the bond between the two of you. If what you are doing annoys or hurts your dog, stop doing it! That seems simple, but you may be so sure that your dog is going to enjoy the massage that you may miss him telling you he doesn't. Also, massage is no substitute for veterinary care.

Chiropractic

Chiropractic treatment may also help your dog, especially if you and he are very active. An adjustment may be just what your Dachshund needs to keep zipping around that agility course. Find a veterinarian who not only offers chiropractic services, but will also know if some other form of treatment is needed.

While you may not feel comfortable with every type of alternative or traditional veterinary care, you may come to appreciate a veterinarian who is willing to try all forms of treatment to give the best health care to his patients. So many alternatives are, in fact, complementary to traditional medicine.

SENIOR YEARS

As your friend ages with you and your family, pay particular attention to his physical and mental needs. Just like us, animals are affected by age in many ways. Not only will you find your Dachshund sleeping more and slowing down a bit overall, you'll notice changes in his coat (more white hairs), changes in his skin

Your friend deserves the best care you can give him until the very end.

(thickening in parts, more droop around the eyes, etc.), changes in his senses, and changes in his temperament. He may be less responsive to your calls or body language, and he may be moodier. These are all changes you should take note of and, if any of them become a real problem, consult your veterinarian.

Otherwise, the kind and responsible thing to do is care for your senior citizen as you would any other member of your family— with some additional "tender loving care," including more or

As your Dachshund ages, you will notice changes to both his physical appearance and his behaviour.

fewer blankets in his bed, dietary supplements that may help his joints or vision or mental acuity, and attention to his physical limits (less playtime, shorter walks, etc.).

SAYING GOODBYE

One of the tragedies of loving a dog is that they often die before we do. We want them to live forever, and they want to be with us forever, but this just can't be. And like any death, no matter how

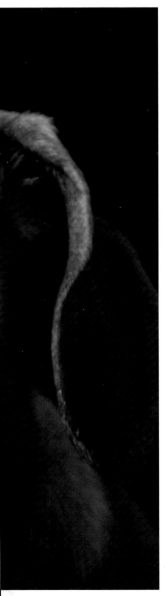

prepared for it you think you may be, each is unique, and each is painful.

Fortunately, we can choose a painless and dignified death for our companion animals, and it's our obligation to do so. If your Dachshund is suffering and you can sense that it is time, you need to pay attention to the situation and do what's best for your friend. Hopefully you won't need to make this decision in an emergency situation, but instead can take a few days or maybe weeks to spend the most quality time possible with him toward the end.

You may want to visit your veterinarian and go over your dog's symptoms and your suspicions. Especially if he's cared for your dog for a long time, your veterinarian will also care deeply about doing what's best. Ultimately, however, the decision needs to be yours and your family's.

If you have the extra time, be grateful and make as many preparations as possible so you won't need to make quick decisions you might later regret when you're overwhelmed with grief. You want to consider whether you'd prefer to have the shot administered at the veterinarian's or at your home; not all vets make house calls to do this, but some do. It's worth finding out!

Another thing to consider is what you want to do with your dog's body when he's gone. You have several options, including cremation. Many animal owners keep their pet's ashes in a special container with a photo or poem beside it. Some can bury their friend on their property. You may simply want your veterinarian to dispose of it. Be sure it's what you want.

When it's really time, however difficult it may be, try to be calm for your friend. Remember, he has spent his life being sensitive to your feelings; he will certainly know that you are very upset and that it's because of him. You want him to feel your love, not your anguish. Surround him with his favourite things—a favourite toy, his softest blanket—and let everyone in the family say goodbye, including other animal friends. In the car or at home, play some relaxing music to help everyone feel more peaceful. You may want to light a candle with a favourite scent. Don't put this too close to your dog, though, as the smell may irritate him and you certainly don't want to risk dripping hot wax on him. Keep the lights low. Anyone who doesn't feel well prefers dim lighting. Sing to your friend if you want to.

Your veterinarian should explain the procedure for giving the shot and how your dog will react. If you don't understand, ask him or her to repeat it. Stay with your friend if at all possible—he needs you to help him to the other side with love. Whisper in his ear, remind him of your favourite times together, hold him close but not too tightly. Let him know how much you love him.

When he's gone, spend as much additional time with his body as you want. After you've taken care of your dog, take care of yourself. Many people say losing a canine companion is even worse than losing a person.

Dogs understand us intimately and love us unconditionally. Their loss is life-changing. Allow yourself to grieve, for as long as it takes. Allow your family to grieve, and notice how the loss of your dog affects the other animals in your household.

Reflect on what was hopefully a long and full life you shared with your dog, and look forward to the time when you'll be reunited.

ASSOCIATIONS AND ORGANISATIONS

Breed Clubs

The Kennel Club (UK)
1 Clarges Street
London
W1J 8AB
Telephone: 0870 606 6750
Fax: 0207 518 1058
www.the-kennel-club.org.uk

American Kennel Club (AKC)
5580 Centerview Drive
Raleigh, NC 27606
Telephone: (919) 233-9767
Fax: (919) 233-3627
E-mail: info@akc.org
www.akc.org

Canadian Kennel Club (CKC)
89 Skyway Avenue, Suite 100
Etobicoke, Ontario M9W 6R4
Telephone: (416) 675-5511
Fax: (416) 675-6506
E-mail: information@ckc.ca
www.ckc.ca

The Dachshund Club (UK)
Secretary: Mrs. A. Moore
E-mail: secretary@dachshundclub.co.uk
www.dachshundclub.co.uk

The Dachshund Club of America
Secretary: Andra H. O'Connell
www.dachshund-dca.org

United Kennel Club (UKC)
100 E. Kilgore Road
Kalamazoo, MI 49002-5584
Telephone: (269) 343-9020
Fax: (269) 343-7037
E-mail: pbickell@ukcdogs.com
www.ukcdogs.com

Federation Cynologique Internationale (FCI)
Secretariat eneral de la FCI
Place Albert 1er, 13B - 6530 Thuin
Belgique
www.fci.be

Rescue Organisations and Animal Welfare Groups

Royal Society for the Prevention of Cruelty to Animals (RSPCA) Telephone: 0870 3335 999
www.rspca.org.uk

British Veterinary Association Animal Welfare Foundation
7 Mansfield Street
London W1G 9NQ
Telephone: 0207 436 2970
Email: bva-awf@bva.co.uk
www.bva-awf.org.uk

Scottish Society for the Prevention of Cruelty to Animals (SSPCA)
Braehead Mains, 603
Queensferry Road
Edinburgh EH4 6EA
Telephone: 0131 339 4777
Email: enquiries@scottishspca.org
www.scottishspca.org

Sports

Agility Club UK Canine
www.agilityclub.co.uk

Freestyle Federation Inc
Secretary: Brandy Clymire
Email: secretary@canine-freestyle.org
www.canine-freestyle.org

International Agility Link (IAL)

Global Administrator: Steve Drinkwater
Email: yunde@powerup.au
www.agilityclick.com

Therapy

Pets As Therapy
3 Grange Farm Cottages
Wycombe Road, Saunderton
Princes Risborough
Bucks HP27 9NS
Telephone: 0870 977 0003
www.petsastherapy.org

Training and Behaviour

Association of Pet Dog Trainers (APDT)
PO Box 17
Kampsford GL7 4W7
Telephone: 01285 810 811

Association of Pet Behaviour Counsellors
PO Box 46
Worcester WR8 9YS
Telephone: 01386 750743
Email:: info@apbc.org.uk
www.apbc.org.uk

British Institute of Professional Dog Trainers
www.bipdt.net

Veterinary Resources

British Veterinary Association (BVA)
7 Mansfield Street
London, England
W1G 9NQ
Telephone: 020 7636 6541
E-mail: bvahq@bva.co.uk
www.bva.co.uk

British Veterinary Hopitals Association (BHVA)
Station Bungalow
Main Road, Stockfield
Northumberland NE43 7HJ
Telephone: 07966 901619
Email: office@bvha.org.uk
www.BVHA.org.uk

Royal College of Veterinary Surgeons (RCVS)
Belgravia House
62-64 Horseferry Road
London SW1P 2AF
Telephone: 0207 222 2001
Email: admin@rcvs.org.uk
www.rcvs.org.uk

Association of Chartered Physiotherapists Specialising in Animal Therapy (ACPAT)
52 Littleham Road
Exmouth, Devon EX8 2QJ
Telephone: 01395 270648
Email: bexsharples@hotmail.com
www.acpat.org.uk

Association of British Veterinary Acupuncturists (ABVA)
66A Easthorpe, Southwell
Nottinghamshire NG25 0HZ
Email: jonnyboyvet@hotmail.com
www.abva.co.uk

PUBLICATIONS

Books

Nester, Mary Ann
Agility Dog Training
Interpet Publishing, 2007

O'Neill
What Dog?
Interpet Publishing, 2006

Harvey, Su
Good Pup, Good Dog
Interpet Publishing, 2007

Evans, J M
What If My Dog?
Interpet Publishing, 2005

Tennant, Colin
*Mini Encyclopedia of Dog Training &
Behaviour*
Interpet Publishing, 2006

Barnes, Julia
Living With A Rescued Dog
Interpet Publishing, 2004

Evans, J M & White, Kay
Doglopaedia
Ringpress Books, 1998

Evans, J M
Book of The Bitch
Ringpress Books, 1998

Magazines

Dogs Monthly
Ascot House
High Street, Ascot,
Berkshire SL5 7JG
Telephone: 0870 730 8433
E-mail: admin@rtc-associates.freeserve.
co.uk
www.corsini.co.uk/
dogsmonthly

Dog World Ltd
Somerfield House
Wotton Road, Ashford
Kent TN23 6LW
Telephone: 01233 621 877

Dogs Today
Town Mill, Bagshot Road
Chobham
Surrey GU24 8BZ
Telephone: 01276 858880
Email: enquiries@dogstodaymagazine.
co.uk
www.dogstodaymagazine.co.uk

Kennel Gazette
Kennel Club
1 Clarges Street
London W1J 8AB
Telehone: 0870 606 6750
www.thekennelclub.co.uk

K9 Magazine
21 High Street
Warsop
Nottinghamshire NG20 0AA
Telephone: 0870 011 4114
Email: mail@k9magazine.com
www.k9magazine.com

Our Dogs
Our Dogs Publishing
5 Oxford Road
Station Approach
Manchester
M60 1SX
www.ourdogs.co.uk

Your Dog
Roebuck House
33 Broad Street
Stamford
Lincolnshire PE9 1RB
Telephone: 01780 766199

DEDICATION

For my family, and for Nikole Knobloch

ABOUT THE AUTHOR

Susan Ewing has been "in dogs" since 1977. She owned and operated a boarding kennel for four years and enjoys showing and participating in various performance events. She is affiliated with the Dog Writers Association of America and the Cat Writer's Association, of which she is treasurer. Susan has been writing professionally since 1964 for newspapers, magazines, and radio. Her column, "The Pet Pen," is in The Post Journal (Jamestown, NY) every Saturday. She currently lives in Mesa, Arizona, with her husband, Jim, and two Pembroke Welsh Corgis, Griffin and Rhiannon.

PHOTO CREDITS

Photos on pages 47, 63, 64, 83, 84, 85, and 108 courtesy of Kathy Bontz

Photo on front cover and photos on pages 18, 78, 79, 87, and 103 courtesy of Paulette Braun

Photos on pages 145 and 193 courtesy of Dan Briski (Shutterstock)

Photo on page 182 courtesy of Dewayne Flowers (Shutterstock)

Photo on page 59 courtesy of Eric Gevaert (Shutterstock)

Photo on page 49 courtesy of Grzegorz Slemp (Shutterstock)

All other photos courtesy of Isabelle Francais and TFH archives